another man's war

The True Story of One Man's Battle
to Save Children in the Sudan

another man's war

The True Story of One Man's Battle to Save Children in the Sudan

Sam Childers

THOMAS NELSON
Since 1798

NASHVILLE   DALLAS   MEXICO CITY   RIO DE JANEIRO   BEIJING

Published in Nashville, Tennessee, by Thomas Nelson. Thomas Nelson is a registered trademark of Thomas Nelson, Inc.

Thomas Nelson, Inc., titles may be purchased in bulk for educational, business, fund-raising, or sales promotional use. For information, please e-mail SpecialMarkets@ThomasNelson.com.

Unless otherwise noted, Scripture quotations are taken from THE NEW KING JAMES VERSION © 1982 by Thomas Nelson, Inc. Used by permission. All rights reserved.

Scripture quotations also taken from HOLMAN CHRISTIAN STANDARD BIBLE. © 1999, 2000, 2002, 2003 by Broadman and Holman Publishers. All rights reserved.

Library of Congress Control Number: 2009921619

ISBN: 9781595551627

Printed in the United States of America

09 10 11 12 13 QW 9 8 7 6 5 4 3 2 1

*To all the amazing,
courageous children of Uganda
and Southern Sudan*

contents

another man's war

The True Story of One Man's Battle
to Save Children in the Sudan

ONE

notes from the front

Death hides in the tall grass of Southern Sudan. What looks like empty landscape can explode in a heartbeat with rebels from the Lord's Resistance Army shooting, slashing, and burning their way through an unsuspecting village. Government officials and NGOs (nongovernmental organizations, like CARE, the United Nations, and the Red Cross) give these renegade soldiers a wide berth; they usually know where the trouble areas are and steer clear of them. Local residents, left to make it on their own, are constantly on edge, always afraid. There are no peaceful nights in the bush. None, that is, except in one place—a forty-acre island of safety and calm in the middle of a hellish, endless civil war. The Shekinah Fellowship Children's Village.

The struggle to keep it secure never stops.

Gunfire crackles here and there outside the perimeter fence day and night. Whenever I travel in the area, I expect to get ambushed. I've had my windshield and my side window shot out. I've had vehicles, including a food truck loaded with groceries for the orphanage, blown up by RPGs. The LRA will shoot at anything, but they're not

1

used to anybody shooting back. They don't expect to be up against a truckload of soldiers with plenty of guns and ammo, which is what they get when they tangle with us on the road.

When I first started driving around in Southern Sudan, my soldiers and I got ambushed all the time. To any normal person that would be a bad thing, but I thought it was great. I went around hoping the LRA would ambush us because every time they did, it gave me another chance to take one of them out—leaving one less LRA soldier to hurt somebody else. Governments can't run and hide forever, and one thing's for sure—negotiating is a waste of time. Who knows how many villagers have been killed while people sit around talking about what a big problem all this is. But when you go out and kill some of the enemy, you're making progress. You're speaking the LRA's language, and suddenly you've got their attention. Less talking and more shooting would bring this whole conflict to an end a lot sooner and save who knows how many lives.

I once got an e-mail from an Irishman who said that when he first started hearing stories about me years ago, he thought I was a myth. He thought some of these reports were pure fiction and that my work in Africa was all a tall tale. I absolutely agree with him; the stories are hard to believe. If you come into Sudan even today, you'll hear what people call myths about this crazy *mzunga* preacher (*mzunga* is the local African word for a white guy). As unbelievable as the myths sound, they're the absolute truth. The important thing to remember, though, is that it was never me doing all these incredible, even miraculous things. It was always God. His power is the driving force behind every victory, every success. He's always with us.

I say "us" because whenever I travel anywhere in Africa, I always have soldiers with me. They are not mercenaries, though the news media often call them that. Frankly I don't care what they call them. These brave members of the Sudanese People's Liberation Army have been trained, equipped, and put under my personal command by the Southern Sudanese government.

Sam with Commander James in 1999

One day I was crossing the border from Sudan into Uganda with two trucks and four well-armed, well-trained troops. We stopped at the border checkpoint. There were a few Ugandan soldiers standing around a dusty little guard shack that needed a coat of paint. A couple of weather-beaten signs instructed drivers to halt at a zebra-striped board blocking the roadway. By this time all the border guards knew me and they didn't make me go through any of the usual paperwork or luggage inspection routine.

As I stopped beside one of the guards, he said, "Pastor, you can't go any further."

"Why not?"

"The LRA is attacking a village just ahead. You must wait until there are enough soldiers to go with you."

"Come on, that's nonsense!" I said, pointing to my squad of uniformed men and at the AK-47 resting in my lap. "We're soldiers. We don't need to wait for anybody."

The guard looked at me with a serious expression. "Pastor, there's over two hundred LRA out there."

Five of us, including me, against two hundred. I liked those odds. I figured each of us was equal to forty of them, so it would work out just about right.

"I'm going," I said. The guard cracked a little smile, shook his head, and took a step back from the truck. He knew he wasn't going to change my mind. As I was about to pull out, I sensed God telling me to prepare for what was ahead. He wanted me to station a soldier named Peter on the roof of the truck with his .30 caliber machine gun. Peter Atem is a tall, regal-looking Dinka.

"Peter," I said, "grab your .30 cal and hop up on the roof." Without hesitation he got out, climbed up, and sat cross-legged, cradling the big .30 cal in his arms. Another soldier sat next to me in the front seat with his AK. I had my AK across my knees with the barrel pointed at the driver-side door; that way I could pick it up and shoot one-handed while driving. Fully automatic, three- and four-shot bursts. I've done it plenty of times.

I put another soldier on the roof of the second truck, then heard God tell me, *You start driving.* I eased off down the road with the other truck close behind. The road was rutted and dusty, so rough that you really couldn't go more than twenty-five or thirty miles per hour, especially if you had a soldier with a machine gun on your roof. Even at that speed sometimes you'd think it was going to shake your liver loose.

But plans for that particular day did not include keeping my liver happy. As we bounced and rattled along, God said, *Drive faster.*

Okay, God, if you say so. I picked up more speed and heard the truck following us rev its engine to keep up.

Faster, God said to me. *Faster. Faster.* And so I drove faster and faster until I thought I couldn't keep control of the wheel. My hefty Land Cruiser was screaming along across the dirt, pounding into ruts, flying over rocks, shaking in midair like a Chihuahua passing a peach pit.

When all four tires went airborne at once, Peter started hollering from up on top. "Pastor! Pastor! I can't hang on any more!" He had one hand gripping his .30 cal and the other through the window opening, braced against the ceiling inside, legs flailing like a bull rider.

Looking ahead I saw a tower of smoke a long way off, billowing up out of the dry brown grass. As we got closer, I could see LRA soldiers chasing villagers across a wavy, heat-distorted scene, flames and smoke roiling out from the burning *tukuls*, the villagers' round thatched huts with mud brick walls. There was chaos and commotion, screaming and moaning from one end of the village to the other.

God spoke to me again. *Tell Peter to start shooting.* Peter was a trained bodyguard and a dedicated soldier. He would do whatever I told him without question. I stuck my head out the window and hollered up at the top of the Land

Cruiser, "Peter, start shooting!" Immediately his .30 cal started spitting fire. The bullets for a .30 caliber are on a big ammo belt that you feed in one side of the chamber. I could hear spent shells flying out of the magazine and hitting the roof of the truck like metal rain—*tink! tink! tink! tink!*

Peter Atem, one of the bodyguards for Sam

As Peter started shooting, I took a glance at my side mirror and saw what I thought must be some kind of optical illusion. Speeding along the road, our two trucks had kicked up a massive cloud of dust that swirled up behind us as high and far as the eye could see. I looked in front of me. When the enemy heard Peter's machine gun fire, they looked at the road and saw the huge dust cloud. They thought a whole army was marching down on them. They turned tail and started running away as fast as their cowardly little legs could take them. I never saw anything close to two hundred soldiers. There were maybe thirty of them, and all I saw were their backs as they ran. The element of surprise allowed us to stop the complete destruction of that village with four soldiers, a *mzunga*, and a cloud of dust.

God protects me in Africa in amazing ways. Sometimes he works long-distance. There are times when I'm in Nimule—the nearest town with such luxuries as electricity and paved roads—and my wife back home in Pennsylvania will wake up to pray for me. She gets out of bed, writes down the date and time, and starts praying. One night God woke her up and told her to go to church and pray. When she got to church, there was another member of our church already there who said God woke her up too and told her to come to the church and pray. The two of them prayed, "God, hide them from the enemy," not knowing where my soldiers and I were at that moment or what we were doing.

Looking at Lynn's prayer journal later, we realized she and her friend were praying exactly at the time my soldiers and I were in an area where the LRA had just staged an ambush. As we arrived, we saw to our amazement that the LRA was rooted in place alongside the road. They could have attacked us by surprise, but they didn't move. Some of them were actually face down in the dirt. You could see them shaking, hiding their faces. They were scared to death, and they wouldn't be that scared of us. I believe what happened that day was they were getting ready to ambush us (and would have killed us in a heartbeat), but God had a mighty army of giant angels traveling with us. I believe that these LRA soldiers saw those angels and trembled in fear of them as we drove by. Those cowards never lifted a finger. You can believe it or not, but that's exactly what happened.

That has actually happened more than once. Another

time we were again driving in an area where the LRA was everywhere. A soldier named Thomas and two other soldiers were with me. We had three AKs inside of the vehicle and that was it; this time we were way outgunned. We were driving as fast as we could to get through this war zone. We came around the corner, and there they were—LRA soldiers walking the road single file. I said to myself instantly, "Oh God! Oh God!"

But all of a sudden it was as if we were driving by these guys in slow motion. We felt like we were on *Matrix* time. As we got closer, they didn't look up at the sound of our engines. Instead, their faces were down and they looked at the ground. They were on the road directly in front of us. It was impossible that they didn't see and hear us. Yet they never looked up except for some who looked in another direction away from us. I looked at Thomas in slow motion and said, "Thomas, these are LRA." He looked at me as scared as could be and said, "Yes, Pastor. Keep praying." We drove by these men, and they never looked up once. We should have been pinned down and had a nasty firefight on our hands. Instead, we drove by completely unnoticed.

I've been ambushed so many times that the stories run together, but I can tell them all day. In another instance, we came around a turn in the road and stopped. Probably a hundred yards or so away were LRA soldiers lying on the road with two .30 cals on tripods. As I got out of the car, the Holy Spirit instantly spoke to me. *Grab your gun.* I reached on the seat and grabbed my AK. I didn't have a shell in the chamber, so I slammed it back and loaded a round. As soon as that shell went into that chamber, all hell broke out.

Everything went into slow motion again. (Before I got used to being ambushed, I felt that sensation a lot.) I started running, heading for a little gully alongside the road and emptying my clip before I got there. I dove into the hole and pulled the empty clip out; I always tape two clips together end to end so I can change them faster. I was so nervous and shook up I couldn't get my full clip back in the gun. I looked up and saw my SPLA soldiers jumping off the vehicles, then walking down the center of the road toward the enemy, firing automatic bursts as they went. I was in my gully hole scared to death, trembling. I hollered at the guys and thought, *Oh my God, my men are all gonna get killed, and the LRA soldiers are gonna capture me and torture me.* A white guy would be a trophy catch, and they would make the most of the opportunity.

My squad kept walking down the center of the road firing their AKs, blanketing the roadway with lead. They'd empty a clip, pull it out, throw it over their shoulder, slam another clip in, and resume fire, walking the whole time, never slowing down. Finally the enemy broke and ran. None of our guys was hurt. Afterward I remember a crazy thought going through my head: *We think Rambo was a fighting machine. These SPLA soldiers are the real Rambo.*

So many times my experiences remind me of how one person can make a difference, and I find I need reminding from time to time. When you look at me and our tiny operation it's easy to think, *That ragtag little outfit can't help anybody.* Life proves otherwise. One time we came into a village on the Juba Road that had just been raided. Small fires were still burning here and there. The smoky air carried the sharp stench of burning flesh and the cries of the wounded calling out weakly for help. Some of the victims had collapsed along the road trying to escape and lay dying in pools of their own blood. Too far gone to talk, they spoke worlds with their vacant, hopeless eyes.

We heard a commotion and saw a cluster of LRA around a young woman not far off. I thought all the rebels had turned tail and run. This bunch had been too busy to notice we'd arrived, but as soon as they looked up and saw us, they ran too.

The woman was exhausted, hysterical, gasping for breath, and drenched in blood. The soldiers were cutting her breast off with a machete and had about halfway finished the job. She was badly butchered and had obviously lost a lot of blood. We covered her wounds as well as we could, carried her to our truck, and drove her to the hospital in Nimule. Once I knew they would take care of her, I left with the soldiers to continue our patrol.

Probably a year later I was preaching at a church in Maryland, talking about my African ministry. After the service someone in the congregation came up to me and said, "I want to ask you something. Do you really think you can make a difference?" His question stunned me into silence. "I want to know," he continued, "because I think it's stupid. It's crazy for you to be wasting your time over there in Africa. One person. How can you make a difference?" I couldn't think of what to say, so I didn't say anything.

But his question got me to thinking. After I got home I

got into an argument with God. "You know what, God, this *is* stupid! Here I am working thousands of miles away from my family. My daughter's growing up without me. I have a beautiful wife I'm never with. My family doesn't get the attention and support they deserve and have a right to expect. This is stupid, Lord, because I'm not going to make a difference."

About two weeks after I straightened God out on that, I was back in Nimule. An attractive young lady—a complete stranger—came running up to me on the street, all happy and bubbly, and started hugging me. She was doing her best to communicate with me in her broken English.

"Pastor, do you remember who I am?"

She had me stumped. "No," I said, "I don't really remember you."

"I'm that lady that was in the village when the LRA raided it. They were cutting my breast off, and you and your men saved me." Instantly it was like God said to me, "One man *can* make a difference."

Since that day there is nothing anyone could ever say to convince me that one person cannot change a nation. One person can do unbelievable things. All it takes is that one person who's willing to risk everything to make it happen.

Most of the work my ministry and my soldiers do—and therefore most of the fighting we do—is in Southern and southwestern Sudan. But I've been to other parts of the country, including Boma in southeastern Sudan, a good three hundred miles from where I spend most of my time. It would be about an hour's drive from the Ethiopian border if there were a road to the Ethiopian border, which there doesn't seem to be. For centuries the area has been equally famous for its nomadic cattle herders and the notorious cattle thieves who prey on them. A man's wealth is measured in cattle, and the long-established tradition is to increase your herd any way you can, including stealing cattle and killing your rivals.

Most of the cattle raiders are from the Toposa tribe. They are some of the meanest people I've ever met. These are the Africans you may have seen pictures of that are into body stretching with wooden discs in their lips. In some areas only the women have the discs, and in others men and women both have them. Mothers will make a little hole at the base of a baby's lower lip with a thorn, and enlarge it over time into a hole big enough to put a little wooden plug in. After that, the plugs are replaced with gradually larger ones until finally they can be bigger around than the woman's head. In some tribes a woman's dowry is based on the size of her lip disc. An inexpensive wife might cost ten cows, where one with the biggest lip ring might fetch seventy-five cows, a king's ransom in Boma.

The women there also may have beautiful gold ankle cuffs, bracelets, and other jewelry. There's lots of gold in Boma. So much, in fact, that the tribes there trade it for sugar. Yes, you can go to some places in the Boma region and buy gold with sacks of sugar. Even some of their weapons are gold. The men melt gold or steel into little bracelets an inch around that might weigh a pound or two. That way, when they get into a fight, they don't have to make a fist. They just start swinging their arms and they've got these steel or gold weights around their arms or wrists to take care of business.

12

The women typically wear animal skins and are very beautiful except for having their lips and ears stretched out. The men are usually naked except for bandoleers draped across their chests and AK-47s in their hands.

The Boma Plateau is desert, yet somehow the people have managed to graze cattle for generations. It would be like living and raising cattle in the Nevada desert. The cows are hearty, bony animals with square silhouettes—not sleek at all, but rangy like a Texas longhorn. They have huge horns, however, that are pointed more upward than out to the side like a longhorn. For the raiders, a day's work consists of nothing but robbing people. They will rob you, they will kill you, because that's just what they do. They steal cattle from each other. Whole towns in the region are fenced in with trees of thorns for protection. In the desert certain types of acacia trees grow; they have no leaves but only thorns about as long as a finger and as sharp as a needle.

I was riding with four SPLA soldiers through a section of Boma thick with cattle raiders. In the rainy season, there's so much rain that low places turn into riverbeds running through the desert. We'd been tearing along in this one bed and came up out of it onto an old road that's barely traveled. There in front of us, fifteen or twenty armed raiders had the road blocked. Thomas was driving, flying along fast, and slammed to a halt. All five of us were loaded. I had my AK on my lap as usual. As soon as we stopped, every one of the raiders rushed up and pointed their guns at us in the truck.

Something about the cattle raiders you learn when you're there for a while is that they never have a lot of ammo.

They hardly ever have a full clip in their guns. They'll keep what little ammo they have in belts around them, but usually there are only five or six bullets in the gun. They weren't expecting us to be soldiers; they thought we were just missionaries or some other typically easy, defenseless target. Once they saw what they had hold of, they started hollering back and forth to each other.

One of the soldiers sitting behind me was named Nineteen. He always carried pineapple grenades, which send fragments of metal flying everywhere when they blow. It was so bad that day that Nineteen grabbed a grenade off his belt and pulled out the pin. He was ready for action. (As long as you hold the handle down, a grenade won't blow, even with the pin out. Pulling the pin is the first step. If you don't release the handle you can reinsert the pin. Once you release, the jig's up.)

I could hear these guys talking broken English and once again thought, *I'm going to be the first one shot. I'm the only white guy here. I know everyone's going to shoot me. I've got to shoot this guy in my window. I've got to shoot this guy!* Something inside me kept saying, *Take him now! Take him now!* As the bandits argued, my gun sat out of sight on my lap pointing out the window. I raised my leg nearest the door so I would hit the guy about in the chest or below the chin. I pulled the safety off. I could understand what they were saying. They were speaking different languages, but it all went back to Arabic: "No, let them shoot first. Let them shoot."

My soldiers were trying to talk to them at the same time. I felt it was time to make a move. I started to squeeze the trigger. I was going to shoot this raider right in the throat before somebody shot me. It felt like the longest trigger pull in history. My AK didn't fire and didn't fire, and then I heard one of the raiders say in Arabic, "Okay, we won't fight today." I relaxed my finger, not believing my gun hadn't fired at that exact instant. Nineteen carefully eased the pin back into his pineapple, and we continued on our way.

I should have died in ambushes a hundred times. Some of those times, I didn't even know I was being ambushed. We were going through an LRA area once, and Peter kept grabbing hold of me and pulling me down as we were walking. I couldn't figure him out. That night we were all sitting around at the compound talking about what had happened that day, and Peter was mad at me. Peter is hard to understand when he tries to speak English. He was telling me, "Pastor, you're no good. You're no good. The Bible says thou shalt not test the Lord thy God." He was rattling on and on and finally I said, "Peter, what are you talking about?"

He said, "You're walking today and the people are shooting at you and you just keep walking. The Bible says it's wrong."

"Peter, I didn't know anybody was shooting at me."

"Yeah, Pastor, they were shooting at you."

All I could do was laugh, and the rest of the men joined in. I didn't know the enemy was shooting because I never heard it. My hearing is pretty terrible. I drove construction equipment for years, and I blame some of my hearing loss on that. But I believe a lot of it is from the bombings. I was in bombings in Sudan that made my ears ring for three days. Even now I can't hear a cell phone ringing, so I keep mine on vibrate. Getting older doesn't help matters any. It's getting bad when you think your cell phone's vibrating and you reach for it and it's not there—it's just your body going numb.

Even in the middle of all the fighting and danger, little moments and thoughts come around that lighten our days. There was a time when I'd had it with people ambushing our food trucks, so I came up with a plan. I was going to dress all my soldiers up as women—put dresses on them and tie their guns under their dresses—and let them travel through the bush with sodas and beer on the truck. The LRA wouldn't shoot to kill because naturally they would want the women for sexual pleasure, but when they stopped them, those dresses would come up and they'd have a problem on their hands.

I planned that countermove for the longest time, and then the ambushes slacked off. One day I swear I'll use it.

TWO

whatever it takes

Nimule is three miles or so down a stray ribbon of choking red dirt that passes for a road in Southern Sudan. There isn't much to the place once you get there—a few streets lined with concrete and tin buildings, a cluster of stores, electric lights here and there, a tangle of bicycles, motor scooters, and tired-looking old cars and trucks bobbing around people and animals in the road. But at least you have the sense you're somewhere.

I, on the other hand, was nowhere: a patch of ragged, untamed scrub and underbrush without a sign that man had ever been there. This was the grassland version of the African jungle from the Tarzan movies. Instead of a canopy of leaves and long grape vines to swing on, I was surrounded by acacia trees, tall grass, and matted tangles of weeds. Underfoot was a world-class collection of critters that sting, bite, and pinch, including scorpions, spiders the size of my hand, and some of the deadliest snakes on earth.

A hundred yards away, a little finger of the White Nile flowed north, just starting its long meander from Lake Victoria in the heart of Africa all the way to Cairo and the Mediterranean. Though there were mountains rising up a dusty, hazy purple in the distance, the land around me was flat, so the river moved slowly, whirring and burbling along in no hurry, which is the way most of Africa is.

I hacked away enough brush to lay out my sleeping mat and hang my mosquito net from a tree branch. Sunset comes fast this close to the equator, and I wanted to get settled before dark. A breeze from the river stirred up the still, heavy air that had been baking all day in the tropical sun. Afternoon temperatures routinely top 110 degrees in Southern Sudan, but the nights are mercifully cool. Stretch-ing out on my mat that first night, I looked up through the netting at the stars. I don't know if there are actually that many more stars in Africa than anywhere else or if it just looks that way. The sky is so dark and smooth and clear it makes the stars sparkle like diamonds on black leather, glowing softer and fainter as you drift off to sleep.

From sound asleep to trembling with an adrenaline rush took no more than a heartbeat. The first sensation I had was a big, rough hand over my mouth. I opened my eyes and looked into the face of a Dinka warrior inches from my own, his clan marked by bold, shiny scars cut into his forehead like sergeant stripes. It was Ben, my bodyguard, assistant, and friend, who'd been sleeping a few steps away. With one fluid motion he reached up and cut down my mosquito net with his knife, then held his finger to his lips. We lay motionless side by side on the ground, holding our breath, trying not to make a sound. I hadn't heard whatever Ben had as a warning, but I heard them now, a rhythmic rustling sound coming from the tall, dry grass. Following his eyes in the direction of the river, I saw dim outlines rimmed in moonlight. The Lord's

Resistance Army. Forty, maybe fifty soldiers leaning forward, walking quickly, efficiently through the underbrush lugging weapons, ammo, and supplies.

These were the crazed—some said demon-possessed—rebels who'd been terrorizing northern Uganda and Southern Sudan for years with bloody raids on isolated villages, attacking men, women, and children alike with animal brutality, disfiguring them with machetes, burning them alive, forcing acts of cannibalism. Some of the uniformed shapes were too small to be soldiers. Those would be the children, kidnapped, brainwashed, and forced to mimic the deadly work of their captors.

Which is why I was there.

Though I wasn't exactly prepared for a firefight, I'd faced longer odds plenty of times. One thing about life on the edge with God is that you're fearless. Might as well be. There's nothing to lose because you've already given it all away.

I only had two weapons with me, but they'd gotten me through more tight spots than I could count: a well-worn Bible and a well-oiled AK-47, Russian made, reliable, and good for six hundred fully automatic rounds a minute. As quietly as possible, I rolled over and cradled the AK, flicked off the safety switch with my right thumb, and waited. Ben had his AK too. We watched the troops go by, saw the last one disappear through the tall grass, then listened for a long minute. All we heard was the river in the distance and the insects and night animals all around. When we were sure the last soldier was gone, Ben went back to his spot, and I retied my net, stretched out on my mat, and drifted back toward sleep watching those incredible stars.

The first time I saw that scruffy patch of land was on my third trip to Africa, driving a mobile clinic that brought medicine to people in the bush displaced by the LRA. I had seen refugees in one remote village that were so sick and felt God calling me to start a medical ministry to them. I said, "Okay, God, I'll do it, but you're going to have to come up with the truck." The next time I was back home in America, I tried to raise some money for the project, but only collected about a thousand dollars. A few days before I was supposed to go back to Sudan, my wife phoned me on the road and said a man had called to ask how much the mobile clinic would cost. She told him thirty-three thousand dollars.

The man and I talked on the phone, and he said he wanted to give me the balance of what I needed. He asked, "How much do you have left to raise?" I told him, "Thirty-two thousand dollars."

That surprised him. He said, "I thought you were collecting donations."

"We are," I explained, "but so far we've only got a thousand."

He didn't plan on donating so much money to the cause, but he was a man of his word. I didn't know this guy, had never seen him before in my life, but he met me at the Washington airport and gave me thirty-two thousand dollars cash in a paper sack. With that miraculous windfall we were able to buy a safari vehicle, an overgrown white Land Cruiser with a big sunroof and benches in the back with room for thirteen people to squeeze in.

A lot of displaced people in the bush couldn't walk to town to see a doctor. Their homes had been burned by the

LRA, their families killed and maimed. The local relief agencies were afraid to send medical help for fear of more rebel attacks. There's no doubt it was a dangerous place to be. I organized trips with the Land Cruiser to bring medicine to the villages, even though as a *mzunga* I was a prize target for rebel sharpshooters.

Once in a while, we had doctors or nurses from the U.S. helping us as volunteers, but most of the time the medical teams I took in were Sudanese locals. We always had several of my soldiers with us too, both for our own protection and to safeguard the villagers who came to see us. Where there were roads, we drove into settlements and set up under the trees, working out of the back of the Land Cruiser as people crowded around. For the villages we couldn't drive to, we got as close as we could and then the workers carried the supplies the rest of the way, sometimes up to two miles. We had four big rectangular metal boxes about two feet deep painted red with black tops and "Mobile Clinic" written on the sides. Inside each one was a stack of trays with medicines and supplies, kind of like a giant tackle box. Our Sudanese helpers carried them balanced on their heads. Whether we had medical doctors along or not, we brought all kinds of medicine and equipment—morphine, sutures, you name it. We could do almost anything, and we did, from sewing up gunshot wounds to treating fevers and spider bites. When we had the money, we also brought food with us to give away. We'd give each family who came to see us a couple of scoops of rice or beans.

One day I was driving along outside Nimule when God gave me this sudden powerful feeling that I should stop my car. One of the soldiers with me then said, "What are you doing, Pastor?" I said, "I just want to look around here a little bit."

There was nothing there at the spot but woods and underbrush. At least that's what I saw, but God spoke to me inside my heart. *This is where I want you to build my children's home. Build it here.* The LRA had orphaned thousands of children. They'd kidnapped them and forced them into service as porters, sex slaves, and child soldiers, abducting them from burning villages as they saw their parents hacked with machetes or murdered. When the kids escaped or were rescued, some of them had no families to return to because they were the only ones who'd survived the attack. They needed a safe place to live and go to school, a place where they could be kids without worrying about getting attacked or abducted. A place to help them piece their lives back together and look with hope toward the future.

And this was the place God had chosen for them.

I, however, had no plans whatsoever for a children's home in Africa. I was busy running a mobile clinic. I was also a pastor with a wife and daughter back in Pennsylvania and a church to lead. I had no financial support for a children's home, and no idea where to start.

God said, *Start here.*

I found out who owned the land. I had hoped it was government property because then I could probably lease it for next to nothing, but it turned out it belonged to a wealthy old man in town named Festus, whose family had farmed hundreds of acres of land and grazed their cattle on it for generations. I went to see him and asked if I could buy the forty acres I'd seen.

"This land has been in my family for hundreds and hundreds of years," he said, "but yes, I will sell it to you."

When the local authorities learned that I'd bought the land, one of the officials came to me and said, "Pastor, the LRA will kill you out here! They come through this area all the time. Build your project in Nimule where it's safer." All the NGOs in the region were set up in town.

"No," I said, "I can't do that. God wants his children's home here, and this is where I'm going to put it. He will protect us."

The official's remark reminded me of what my dad always used to say: "Boy, somebody's gonna kill you one of these days."

Maybe one day they'll both be right, but not while I've got work to do.

I went home to Pennsylvania and told my church and my family about the plan. I think they were shocked by the scope of the project, considering we had no clue how to do it and no resources to do it with. But by that time I'd been springing African schemes on them for years, and they were sort of used to it.

Two months later I was back in the bush to camp out on the land and start clearing it. When I got to Nimule, a soldier named Ben William came to see me. As I said earlier, his lanky build and coal-black skin identified him as a Dinka, a prominent tribe in Southern Sudan. He also sported the decorative scars his people have, often made bolder by rubbing ashes in the cut. I'd met Ben earlier in another part of Sudan, and he heard I was coming to build a home for the war orphans. Not knowing when I'd be back, he stayed in town, sleeping out in the open and just getting by from day to day, confident that I'd return. He found out I was there and looked me up.

This tough, fearless soldier gave me a big hug and said, "Pastor, I'm here to be your servant." And that was it. He scarcely left my side from then on. We drove out to the land I'd bought with a Bible, a mosquito net, and a couple of AK-47s. The first night we were there was when the LRA came through. Rebels or no rebels, we had a job to do. The next morning, Ben and I grabbed some hand tools and started clearing the tall grass. Once we had enough space we built ourselves a *tukul*. These houses are maybe ten or twelve feet across and you can build one in four days or so. If you make a fire inside, it's smoky all the time because there's no chimney or even a hole in the top. The smoke drifts up and works its way through the thatched roof. From outside it looks as though the whole thing is on fire.

Once we finished the first *tukul*, we just kept clearing, going in a circle and making the area bigger and bigger. I got the master plan of the whole thing one night in a vision. I saw exactly what it would look like when it was finished, with a school, a clinic, dormitories, a kitchen, a library, and all the rest.

How could one American pastor and one sergeant in the Sudanese People's Liberation Army possibly do anything like that?

They couldn't. But with God everything is possible.

Even now I can see that first *tukul* in my mind, see the

tree where my mosquito net hung from over the grass sleeping mat. When I look at what's there now I start to cry tears of joy. People today see our Children's Village in person, on our Web site, or on a DVD or TV show and can't imagine that it started with a mosquito net hanging in a tree.

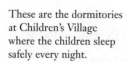

These are the dormitories at Children's Village where the children sleep safely every night.

There's no way it would have happened without Christ. No way.

Building an orphanage was definitely a long way from what I had in mind when I started going to Africa. I hadn't come there originally to help the children. I'd come to do some roofing work in a town up the road. But one young child, whose name I'll never know, changed my plans. And my heart. And the course of my life.

The first trip I took to Sudan was near the end of 1998, after I heard a white South African pastor speak at our church about his plan to train chaplains for the Southern Sudanese army. Except for a few years during the 1970s and '80s, Sudan has been at war with itself since 1955. The Arab Muslim north has forced its religion and culture on the south, which is mostly Christian or local African religions. The majority of the people and power have always been in the north, hammering away at the six million non-Muslims in the south and trying to make them convert to Islam. According to some tallies, as many as four million people have been driven from their homes during the decades of fighting, and two million killed. Two million.

In 1983 a Sudanese lieutenant colonel named John Garang, who'd gone to college in Iowa and studied military tactics at Fort Benning, Georgia, rebelled against his own government in Khartoum and formed the Sudanese People's Liberation Army. This army defended people in the south who didn't want to be Muslims. Though Garang and many of the other SPLA leaders were Christians, they didn't try to force their faith on anybody. They weren't—and aren't—fighting for Christianity; they're fighting to give people the freedom to worship any way they want to. This includes freedom to serve Christ, but it also includes freedom to follow their own local religion or no religion at all.

The SPLA wanted Christian chaplains, so the provisional government of Southern Sudan gave a South African pastor a bombed-out college compound to convert into a military chaplain school. The ruined buildings were in Yei, about a hundred miles west of Nimule as the sand grouse flies, though it's a lot farther on the ground. Making the drive, there are some mountains to the south that you can see out the left side of the car, but other than that it's a red dirt path through a grassy plain stretching to the horizon in every direction. In the dry season—spring and summer—your car kicks up a rooster tail of dust that hangs in the air and gets on and in everything. When the rains come, you go the whole way in four-wheel drive and hope the ruts don't get too deep. The clay soil is slick as glass when it's wet, so if you don't get stuck, you slide all over the place. You have to carry all your gas, water, food, and anything else you might need. There's no town between Nimule and Yei, and if there's a building on the way, I can't remember it.

Yei is a lot like Nimule—red dirt roads, concrete and tin buildings, plenty of people on foot, and bicycles everywhere. And it's just as hot. At four degrees latitude above the equator, the sun broils everything, bleaches the sky white, and evaporates the clouds. The old college buildings there were bombed out and torn apart, really in rough shape. At that time in my life, I was a building contractor who'd been walking with the Lord for six years. This South African pastor asked me if I'd volunteer to help put new roofs on these buildings and do some other fixing up. I had never been to Africa in my life, never even thought about it. But I felt God calling me to go, so I said yes.

Five weeks later, I was in Yei. The old school buildings there were so broken apart we couldn't stay in them at first, so we lived in a compound down the street run by the Catholic Church. I got the crew started at putting up steel and making repairs. I found an old welding machine that barely worked and used it to build a new front gate from junk pieces of steel lying around. In the end it wasn't bad looking, and I guarantee it was solid. I fixed the bullet holes in the water tower and repaired the water pump where all the gaskets were rotted away. In the best of times there's never much money in Sudan for preventive maintenance. Considering the heat and dust and rain—and the fact that people had been shooting up the place for fifteen years—it's a wonder anything worked at all.

While we were there, the shooting and bombing went right on. Sometimes we'd hear the whine of government bombers in the distance, drop our tools, run outside, and jump in a hole that was the closest thing they had to a bomb shelter. One time the radical Muslims bombed only a block or so from where we were staying. Even at a distance, the sound is deafening, rocks and pieces of whatever the bomb hit fly through the air, and the ground shakes. If you're lying on the ground, you feel it in your whole body. I thought to myself, *This is what the people here live with, year after year, never knowing when the next strike will come, or the next wave of soldiers with torches and machetes.*

The thing that turned five weeks in Yei into a lifetime mission in Africa for me was a metal disc about the size of a dinner plate. Radical Muslims had planted land mines all over the area, like they have in so many other places in Sudan. These Vietnam-era mines are cheap, reliable, and easy to use; and once they're in the ground, they stay armed indefinitely, which is what makes them so dangerous to the local population. Northern armies plant them by the thousands just below the surface to maim SPLA soldiers. But once the fighting moves on, nobody comes back to clear the area. Setting them out is relatively safe and easy, but removing them once they're armed is a very dangerous job, so they just leave them in the ground. These northern troops even set out minefields in places soldiers don't typically go in hopes of injuring innocent civilians as part of their campaign of intimidation and terror.

The road to Juba, miles and miles of which are still under construction to remove land mines

Coming into town, there were places where I saw the bodies of people killed by mines or massacred by soldiers. Not bodies really, just skeletons. Between the climate and the scavengers, dead flesh doesn't last long, though even at that, the sick-sweet smell of rot hung in the air. In one massacre outside of town, five thousand people were killed. Skeletons were heaped on top of skeletons. You could feel death in the air.

The mines around Yei are a combination of antipersonnel mines and larger antitank mines, a handful of the more than one million scattered around the world, as dangerous fifty years later as the day they were set. The battle advances, markers and warning signs disappear, and people eventually forget the mines are in the ground until it's too late. They're not designed to kill, but to cripple. A dead soldier is a dead soldier, but a wounded one slows down his whole unit and diverts the focus temporarily from attacking and moving to medical treatment. So the antipersonnel mines are sized to blow off a foot or shatter a leg.

Assuming the victim is an adult. With boots.

One day I was walking through an area where a lot of people had lost their lives. Women, older people, anybody barefoot or wearing sandals could be killed. Nobody had come looking for these victims—probably because the rest of the family was already dead—and there's no sort of organized government program for collecting the bodies, so they pile up around the minefields. Awful as it is, the sight is a very effective reminder to the living to be careful. I was with some of the other workers, walking along and looking at the mangled corpses, when we came across the body of a child. From the waist down there was nothing. I couldn't tell if it had been a boy or a girl. The lower half was just gone.

I stood over that little body, looking down at what had once been a precious child—playing, laughing, full of life and energy and hope, too young to despair, too young to hate. Running through this spot no more than a few days ago, per-haps playing a game? Finishing an errand? Chasing a pet? That child put a dusty, grubby little foot on a pressure cap that triggered a small explosive charge. There was a *pop!* and a flash that lasted only a second. But by the time it was over, the child was already dead and dismembered. One more anonymous casualty out of millions.

I started to weep. I couldn't stand to look at it, and yet I couldn't turn my head. The image blurred, then cleared again, as tears filled my eyes and spilled down my face.

"I will do whatever I have to do to help the people of Sudan."

It was my voice but it didn't feel like the words were com-ing from me.

"Lord, I tell you now, I'll do whatever I have to do to help these people. These children. I'll do it! Whatever it takes, Lord! Whatever it takes!" I kept saying the same thing over and over. "Whatever it takes. Whatever it takes." Some presence had a hold of me in that moment that would change my life from then on. I didn't know what the change would look like or how it would happen. All I knew was that it was there.

But how could that be possible? I owned a construction company and business was booming. I owned rental property and land. Against very long odds, Sam Childers, high school dropout and former drug dealer, had grabbed a piece of the American dream. Yet standing over half of a tiny body outside a dirt-road town in the middle of an African plain halfway around the world, suddenly none of that mattered.

My first day home back in the States, I went to my mom's for breakfast. Even though I'd been married for years, it was kind of a tradition for me to have breakfast with Mom several mornings a week since Dad passed away. She lived across the street from me in the house where I'd lived as a boy, a trailer my dad had hauled to the site then added rooms and a permanent roof to, all painted bright white and accented with a big, black-and-white checkerboard design on the garage doors. I was sitting at the kitchen table where I'd sat hundreds of times before, surrounded by all the familiar sounds and smells of a home-cooked breakfast on the way. But my mind was a long way off.

Mom looked over at me. You can't fool a mom. She asked, "Sam, are you okay?"

I tried to answer, but the words wouldn't come. I broke down in tears. Finally I managed, "No, I'm not."

She didn't say anything else; just sat down by me and let me cry awhile. Then she asked softly, "What's wrong?"

I looked over at her, red-eyed, and said, "I think I left a piece of me in Africa." And I put my face down on her shoulder and sobbed like a child.

THREE

a lot of stuff

"Boy, somebody's gonna kill you one of these days!"

From the time I was a boy until just before he died, my dad probably told me that a thousand times. He didn't say it in a serious way—sometimes it came out almost like a joke, even though it had some bite to it. It was his shorthand way of telling me I was tenacious, tough, mean, and either too brave or too stupid to be afraid of anybody. That sort of focus and drive can be a great tool for achieving success, if success is your goal. It can also be a great tool for immorality, mischief, and high-impact hell-raising if that's what you're after, which was the choice I preferred in my youth. I'd heard stories about Dad's early days, the boxing and his hitch in the Marine Corps, and I wanted to be like what I thought he was. Turns out that I got it all twisted up, though I don't think he ever knew how far off track I went.

Paul Childers was a Christian man who worked hard and fought hard. He was my hero. He quit school in the third grade to make money during the Depression. His mother, a Cherokee Indian, died when he was about five, and his father died a few years later. So from the time he was fourteen or so, he raised himself. He hopped a freight train to Florida and learned a trade. As a union ironworker for more than fifty years, he always had a job in good times and bad because he would work harder than anybody else. He was medium height with thick arms and a solid build. He had dark hair and a square face with deep-set eyes, a no-nonsense mouth, and the broad nose and prominent cheekbones of his mother's Cherokee ancestors.

Dad met my mother when she was seventeen and he was about twenty-eight. It wasn't until near the end of his life any of us knew he'd been married before, but he was like that—very private about his personal history. Mom and Dad moved from place to place following the big construction projects. I was born in Grand Forks, North Dakota, where Dad was working on a missile plant. I think they made Minuteman nuclear ICBMs there, or maybe it was an underground installation where they kept them on alert during the Cold War. I had two older brothers, Paul Jr. and George. After George I had a sister, Donna, but she died of a heart problem before she was a year old. Dad took her death hard, but being Dad he just kept on working, even though sometimes at night he would hold her pajamas in his arms and cry and cry. Mom had a nervous breakdown. She was so eaten up by what she lost that she couldn't be a mom to the two boys she had.

One day she was looking out the window at my brothers swinging in the yard, and God spoke to her. He reminded her that she had two other children and told her she still had something to live for. Starting then, she began to reconnect with her family and the world around her.

Before they lived in Grand Forks, my family had lived in

Grand Rapids, Minnesota. One day she'd gone to church there, and the pastor prophesied that she would have another child who would be a minister. Not long after that was when they moved, and a pastor in Grand Forks gave her the same prophecy. She went home from church all happy and, as she's always told the story, I was conceived that night. Two other times—once in the womb and again when I was five or six years old—other pastors prophesied that I would be a preacher. Through the years, my mother always held on to those prophecies, even at times when people with less faith would have long since thrown in the towel.

I couldn't have been more than about nine years old when I felt God's hand on me for the first time. It was at my great-grandmother's funeral at the old Assembly of God church in Central City, Pennsylvania, where we were living by then. It bothered me to see all those people crying over my great-grandmother and missing her so much. They seemed so lost and so sad. I had gone into the bathroom and was looking at myself in the mirror. At that moment I said to God, "I want to help these people. I don't want them to feel like this." I remember the compassion I had for the people at that moment, how strongly I felt it and how real it seemed. Somehow I knew that mourners could make it through the pain and loss, and that somehow I could help them do that. As much wrong as I did later in life and as many people as I hurt, I can say that God never stopped talking to me. I just stopped listening.

In the spring of 1974, a couple of months before I turned twelve, we moved back to Grand Rapids. I was going into seventh grade that fall, and the two years between then and when I started high school were some of the most influential times of my life. That's when I fine-tuned the outlook and the behavior that landed me in the moral and spiritual cesspool where I spent so much of my life. At the time, I loved every minute of it. I know now that if I'd died then or any time for years afterward I would have gone straight to hell.

Before we left Central City, I had already discovered cigarettes, marijuana, and alcohol. The first time I ever smoked pot had surprised my brother George when he was toking in the barn.

"I'm gonna tell!" I shouted, like a typical little kid who got the goods on his older brother.

"Here, take a drag," he said and held out the joint. I hesitated. "Here! Smoke it!" It wasn't an invitation; it was an order. I took a puff.

"Now you've smoked it too. If you tell on me, I'll tell on you!" He had me. Besides, the sensation I got from the smoke was fantastic. It felt really good. Pot was wonderful stuff.

Even though my first experience with illegal drugs came from my brother, I can't blame him for my early attraction to alcohol and pot. I had always liked hanging out with older boys, and part of being accepted was to do what they did. When you're only eleven and the teenagers will let you run with them if you do what they do, you'll do whatever it takes to be recognized as a member of the group.

My family bought a piece of land in Cohasset, outside Grand Rapids, and right away I started meeting a lot of guys in the community. One of my favorite buddies was named

Allen Pierce. He was the same age as me, and we clicked right off the bat. Growing up, I always looked older than I was, which helped me fit in with the older boys I wanted to pal around with. I had an allowance from my parents, plus a job delivering newspapers, meaning there was always plenty of money to buy whatever I wanted. And what I wanted was drugs.

Seventh grade was a blast. It seemed like every day we were smoking cigarettes and pot at school. By the next year I was taking white cross, an addictive amphetamine, or "upper," that came as a white pill with a cross on it. It gave me a boost of energy and kept me awake and wired so I wouldn't miss anything. The same year I also discovered LSD. When I used it, it gave me wild visions of patterns, imaginary animals, kaleidoscopic lights that sparkled and melted, and fantastic out-of-body experiences. My friends and I would spend our time either at the Cohasset baseball field—where we smoked and drank in the dugouts—or under the Mississippi River bridge at the edge of town. Sometimes we slept under the bridge all night, and in the summer we dove off of it.

Neither of my parents knew my brothers and I were into drugs. And they sure didn't know about the sex. I burn with shame now when I think about it. As with pot, I got experience at an early age. My first time, I was not quite fourteen, and she was a grown woman, a neighbor who lived down the street from us. Over the next few years I slept with partners by the dozens, from girls younger than I was up to women who must have been forty or forty-five, middle-aged ladies with families and careers who just wanted to walk on the wild side for a little while. I mowed yards for several of them who lived in our neighborhood, but I entertained them in bed too. I remember more than once Mom taking a phone call and then hollering outside to me, "Sam, Mrs. So-and-so wants to know when you're coming to mow her yard." And I would think, *Oh no! Not Mrs. So-and-so again!* But most of the time I went.

By the time I got to high school, my life was one nonstop party. It's a miracle I didn't get killed. A lot of the people I ran with in those days ended up dead in car wrecks, driving when they were drunk or high or both. When I left high school, I was taking everything I could get my hands on, which was a lot of stuff. I smoked pot constantly. I started shooting up cocaine and heroin, sometimes both at once. When I first took LSD, I swallowed it in a pill, but later on my buddies and I dissolved it in water and shot it up for an instant acid rush. Then we'd keep the buzz going with whatever else we had around. Sometimes it was whiskey, sometimes PCP (we called it angel dust), sometimes amphetamines, sometimes quaaludes (which supposedly enhanced sexual pleasure).

I started dealing drugs, which gave me even more money so I could buy even more drugs. By the time I was sixteen, people were calling me Doc because I could find a vein faster and shoot somebody up quicker than anybody else in town. I gave plenty of people their first hit. I bought a Triumph 750 motorcycle with a chopper frame, using some of my drug profits, though a lot of the time I was too drunk or stoned to even sit on it, much less ride it. I'd gotten my first motorcycle when I was about eight and immediately taught myself to pop wheelies in the front yard. My dad must have bought me six or seven little motorcycles and dirt bikes before I bought my first real one. I've loved bikes ever since, to the point where the biker lifestyle eventually became a major part of who I was.

Besides drugs and sex, the third big thing in my life was fighting. My dad taught me why to fight and how to win; he also taught me a lesson about respect and about taking charge that shaped my view of the world. My dad was a Christian and a good provider who loved his family and followed the Lord the best he knew how. By the time I knew him, he didn't pick fights or go looking for them like he might have once, but he sure would finish them. He couldn't stand to see a helpless person get bullied, and he had no hesitation wading into a situation if he thought somebody was being treated unfairly. I know now that the urge to protect people who can't protect themselves is a lot of what has kept me coming back to Africa over the past ten years. A willingness to fight another man's war. Thanks, Dad, for showing me the way.

One time Dad and I were hauling a pickup-load of manure down the road outside of Cohasset with Dad's friend Herb. There was nothing really wrong with Herb; he was a good guy. But he was a little slow and an easy target for people who wanted to make fun of somebody. Two wannabe bikers riding Hondas came by hollering and cussing at Herb and kicking the door of his truck, making fun of him and trying to run him off the road.

"Just keep going," Dad said. These two guys were scaring Herb, but he did what Dad said and kept driving. They wouldn't let up. They kept yelling and trying to bump us into the ditch. Finally Dad said, "Herb, I guess you better pull over." Herb steered over to the side of the road and stopped.

Dad opened the glove box, pawed around inside for a minute, then pulled out a big monkey wrench. I had an idea what was up. "I'll help you, Dad!" I said, eager to get in on the action.

He stopped still and looked right at me. "You stay in the truck," he ordered. "Don't say nothing, just stay in the truck."

The two hecklers had pulled off the road too, just up ahead of us. When they saw Dad walking toward them, they ran back toward the truck to meet him. The looks on their faces said they were thinking today was going to be their day. After all, Dad was probably twice as old as they were. From my point of view, it appeared that they planned on pounding this old manure-hauling geezer.

They met on the side of the road and we heard a quick *thump! thump!* Before we knew what was happening, both would-be attackers were on the ground with blood running from their heads. Dad turned around and walked back to the truck, a calm expression on his face. He opened the door, tossed the wrench on the dashboard, and said, "Come on, Herb, let's go," like nothing ever happened. We drove on to the house. It was the first example I saw of somebody fighting another man's war. It wasn't long before I had a chance to practice the lesson Dad taught me.

Once I got the hang of it, I practiced fighting a lot. I don't know why I liked to fight so much. Maybe it was because I heard so many stories about my dad being a boxer and being in the Marine Corps and I wanted to show him what I could do, wanted him to be proud of me. Maybe it was that like everything else I liked to do, fighting gave me a rush, especially when the other guy was bigger than me. When I was in the ninth grade, I had a fight with the biggest bully in the school. He stopped swinging for a split second, and I hit him a nice straight one, square in the chin. It knocked him out. Actually it was a lucky punch, and the kid should have beat me to a pulp, but the way it turned out, I won by KO. Word got around that I had knocked out this dude, and everybody was scared to death of me after that. They left me alone, at least for a while.

In high school I couldn't stand to see kids getting picked on. Most of the time when I fought, it was to protect people who couldn't protect themselves. There were four groups of kids at my school: jocks, nerds, hoods, and regulars. I was a hood (short for *hoodlum*), and while we were rough, we didn't pick on defenseless people. It was mostly the jocks who did that, and so it was mostly the jocks I fought with. One day I was walking down the hall and saw one of the school's football gods giving a little nerd a hard time. He hocked a huge clam and spit it right on the guy's locker because he knew the kid was too intimidated to do anything about it. The jock didn't see me, but I saw him.

I came up behind Mr. Football, grabbed him by the neck, and started ramming his face into the locker. Hard. *Wham!* His nose gave way against the metal with a crunching sound. Blood spurted from his face, arcing onto the wall. *Wham!* The blood flowed faster. *Wham!* Still faster. The principal came sprinting down the hall. He also happened

41

to be Mr. Football's father. He marched me to his office and called my dad. I'd been caught fighting in school before, and this time I could be expelled. While we waited for my dad, the principal cussed me out until his face was purple, and I cussed him right back. Dad left work and came down to the school.

When my father walked in the door, the principal quit yelling. Dad asked what happened.

"Your boy's been fighting again," the principal said, fuming. "This time he really roughed up my son. Broke his nose! And my son was completely innocent. Sam hit first."

My dad turned to me. "Tell me what happened."

"He was bullying somebody who couldn't fight back, and I did something about it."

My dad turned to the principal. "Okay, what are you going to do?"

"We're going to suspend him for three days."

"All right," Dad answered. "We'll make sure he does his work at home." Then he stood up to leave and looked at me. "Come on, boy," he said, "we're through here. You done good." I spent the next three days doing my lessons at home.

I was getting a reputation as a tough guy, which meant people wanted to pick fights with me, hoping they could say they'd beaten up Sam Childers. Kind of like being the fastest gun in the West. It's great to be fastest, but the problem is everybody comes gunning for you because *they* want to be the fastest.

I can't even begin to remember all the fights I had, but one example will give you some idea of what most of them were like. It was in the bar at the Sugar Hills ski lodge. I looked a lot older than the fifteen years I was, and didn't have any trouble getting served in bars since the drinking age then was eighteen. The local dogcatcher—a former high school jock and serious bodybuilder named Rock—came in and started to pick a fight with me. Rock was in his mid- to late twenties, more than six feet tall, and a big, tough dude. Beating the tar out of me, even though I was smaller, would give him bragging rights because everybody in town knew I'd never lost a fight. He called me out, and as we were walking over to the dance floor to fight, he hit me hard on the back of the head with his fist. I reached into my pocket and grabbed my Buck knife—a sturdy hunting knife that folds like a pocketknife—and clutched it to give my fist some weight.

I pulled that fist out of my pocket and hit Rock in the eye as hard as I could. Then I kept hitting him again and again in the same place. After about the third wallop, there was blood everywhere, and Rock the jock was on the floor, unconscious.

That was on a Friday night. The next Monday morning Rock's mother called my mother, wanting her to pay Rock's doctor bill. Mom asked her how old her son was. Then I heard her say, "Well ma'am, I'm so sorry that this has happened. I've been telling my son that he has to be nicer to people and hold on to his temper. But ma'am, my son is only fifteen years old, and your son hit first." That pretty much put an end to the conversation.

It didn't take long for word to get around that I had beaten up Rock and beat him good. That enhanced my reputation even more as a guy nobody wanted to mess with. Even people who could have whipped me easily were afraid to tangle with the high school kid who sent Rock to the doctor.

Mom defended me like she always did, even though by that time she was beginning to figure out something weird was going on in my life. She started asking me questions, but I always denied I had anything to do with drinking or drugs. Eventually she knew better than to believe me, but she still never lost sight of the prophecy that I would be a preacher. She held on tight to that future hope.

—

It took a lot of years and a lot of heartache before that future came to be. Yet even in high school and during all the wasted years that followed, my experiences were shaping me and preparing my heart to defend weak, innocent people in Africa who couldn't fight for themselves.

When I came home from that first trip to Southern Sudan in 1998, all I thought about was going back. Those children and their families needed somebody to fight their war for them. But was it *me*? I lived in a completely different world with my own responsibilities and had a family of my own to take care of. How could I ever make the transition from one life to another? I had no clue.

"Boy, somebody's gonna kill you one of these days!" That prediction never came true through all my years as an outlaw. Would it happen on the battlefield of an African civil war? My first trip, I'd gone over as a volunteer roofing contractor. Now I was heading back to fight. I'd fought all my life and loved it, but this was different. This time I was fighting God's battle, and I could feel him pulling me back to that place and those desperate people. My dad had died several years before, but as I made plans to return to Africa, I could hear him saying, "Boy, you done good."

FOUR

never stand away

Like the town around it, the Assembly of God church in Central City, Pennsylvania, is neat, modest, and working class. Set in low rolling hills in the southwestern part of the state, Central City is home to fifteen hundred or so souls, definitely blue collar and overwhelmingly white. The church is low slung and contemporary, with brick walls interrupted by vertical panels of rough stone at intervals all the way around. I was raised in that church but hadn't been a regular attendee for years until one hot, sticky June night in 1992.

That was the night my wife, Lynn, talked me into going to a revival. She was a Christian, I wasn't, and that had bugged me big time. I was basically jealous of Jesus. It was as though Lynn was dedicated to somebody else and not to me. She wouldn't go fishing with me on Sunday mornings any more. Wouldn't go to flea markets. Wouldn't sleep in. And on nights when there was a revival, she wouldn't go out to eat dinner. We used to fight about it. Deep down I knew I was the problem, but I wouldn't admit it. I had to win.

The night I realized for sure that my wife absolutely did love me—and was absolutely right about her faith—was after we'd been fighting hard for a week. I woke up in the middle of the night because I thought I heard something in the house. I looked over and saw Lynn on her knees beside the bed praying for me. I tried to reach out to her but I couldn't move or say anything. It was like I was paralyzed, frozen in place. All I could do was lie there and listen to her pray for hours and hours.

A few months later she convinced me to come to the revival service. Hot as it was, the excited congregation inside the church raised the temperature even higher with their singing, shouting, and praising. I sat on the back row, taking it all in—the congregation singing up a storm, the guest evangelist preaching for all he was worth. As I listened I remembered all those prophecies about me when I was young—that I would be a preacher—and over the last few years, I'd been living what I considered a more Christlike life, even though I wasn't a Christian.

The guest evangelist that week was a white South African of English descent—a big, tall scrapper of a man. During the service he gave an altar call. I sensed God working inside me but didn't know what to do, so I didn't do anything. The preacher walked to the back row where I was sitting and looked straight at me.

"What is wrong with you, man?" he asked.

What kind of question is that? I thought. But there was no denying that something powerful, something outside of me, was working on my heart at that very moment.

I wasn't ready to talk about it. "What do you mean?" I said.

"The power of God is all over you and wants to consume you, and look at you—you're just sitting there, rejecting it!"

I knew he was right. Still, it scared me to think of what a commitment might lead to. I didn't want anybody to know I had these feelings, but this guy could see them in me. Though I didn't want to admit it, I knew what the problem was: me. I didn't want to submit myself to Christ. But that night, sitting on the back row, I did. I gave my heart to the Lord, even though I stayed put in my seat and didn't tell anybody.

The next night I went back, and when the altar call came, I walked to the altar, hands lifted high. At times like that, it's easy to mistake emotions for the power of God. Emotions can be powerful and get you all whipped up, but when it's emotions and nothing else that touch you, your heart is not truly changed. People will sometimes see others visibly moved during a service and say, "Oh look, there's the spirit of God on that person. She just gave her heart to God!" But that's not what happened. It was emotion. My experience that night was not driven by emotion. The key difference is that an emotional transformation is a mile wide and an inch deep, while a Spirit-led change transforms you down to the root of your soul. There's no doubt, no hesitation, no going back.

While I was standing at the altar, so filled with thanksgiving and joy, the preacher came over to me and prophesied that I was going to go to Africa, that it would be during a time of war, and that I would go with him! How crazy was that? I had never been anywhere near Africa and had no interest in going. His making a wild statement like that made me mad. I was ready to bust this guy right in the mouth standing there at the altar.

After the service I bolted for the door, then stood on the sidewalk smoking one cigarette after another and waiting for the pastor to come out. The departing crowd dwindled to a trickle, and finally I saw him walk through the door. In typical Sam Childers fashion, I was very up front about expressing my opinion.

I got right in his face and said, "I want to tell you something right now. Don't you tell me I'm going to Africa!" I was hot. "You can just get that crap out of your head right now." Only I didn't use the word *crap*. "Those people got themselves into that mess, and they can get themselves out."

He just stood there listening to me and shaking his head. When I was through ranting at him, all he said was, "We'll see."

Six years later he talked me into going to Africa to do a roofing job. With him. In a war zone.

—

That first trip in 1998—the trip when I saw the carnage at the edge of the minefield—gave me a sample of what I could expect life to be like over there. Sudanese government soldiers set up unofficial roadblocks all the time. Four or five of them in uniform with their AK-47s stopped trucks and small convoys to steal supplies or demand a "toll" before allowing the travelers to pass. My pastor was driving one night—we weren't supposed to drive at night because it was unsafe—when we got stopped by some drunk soldiers at a roadblock on our way out of Yei. There were three of them: one standing over by a tree, and a couple near our vehicle who started arguing with each other, one with a machine gun slung across his back and the other pointing his machine gun through the truck window at my head.

No doubt he had done this plenty of times to people who had no experience with weapons and no idea how to use one. My guess is I was the first person he ever stopped who knew more about an AK than he did. Once I saw that the safety was on, I grabbed the barrel and yanked it as hard as I could. The soldier busted his forehead on the top of the car—hard—and let go his grip. Blood flew everywhere and smeared across the truck as he fell unconscious to the ground. I pulled the machine gun out of his hands, got out of the car, and advanced on the other two soldiers, who took off into the darkness as fast as they could. As far as I can remember, that was the last time we had trouble at that particular spot on the road.

When I got home from that trip, I couldn't think about anything else but the children over there and how hard their lives were. For years I'd put everything I had into making my construction business bigger and more profitable. I was proud of what I'd done, starting with nothing and now grossing a million dollars a year. I was constantly thinking about how to attract more business, make more money, squeeze more out of every minute. Africa changed all that. I couldn't focus on my business. Didn't even want to. I walked through the day in a trance, disconnected from everything around me, my head and heart brimming with thoughts of Yei—the people there, the destruction and death all around them. Innocence destroyed, hope shattered, the future dark and ominous.

I'd spent years collecting all the material things I thought I needed for living the good life. They'd always meant so much to me, and now they seemed selfish, extravagant, absolutely useless. I had an unbelievable gun collection in my house. Until Africa, looking at all those fine guns gave me joy. One day I walked by the gun cases, stopped in front of one of them, and started to cry. *Why?* I thought. *Why do I have all this?* There were children homeless and starving on the other side of the world, and I had guns that cost two thousand dollars apiece sitting in dustproof cases taking up space.

I started selling them. I started selling anything I could sell. I had an incredible bass boat with a portable phone and a TV, a fish finder, thousands of dollars' worth of tackle. I couldn't look at it. I couldn't look at any of the frivolous toys I had anymore. It shamed me to have them when people were dying in Sudan because they didn't have clean water or mosquito nets. I thought, *I gotta do whatever I can to help these people.*

Three months after I got back from Africa, I was over there again. The pastor I traveled with before was still there working on his chaplain school in Yei. He thought I had come back to help him some more with the buildings, but I said, "Buddy, God sent me here to help the children." I explained to him what I felt I should do, but it turned out he didn't want anything to do with a project if he wasn't in charge. Although I'd helped him with his vision, he didn't want to help me with mine. I was disappointed to see that attitude in a man of God whom I considered to be a friend.

I wasn't sure whether to keep working with him or not,

until he and I were eating one day at his project site and a beautiful Sudanese woman served us some rice. He took a bite, paused, then made a face. Suddenly he popped up from the table and stood face-to-face with our astonished server.

"This rice is no good!" he shouted. It wasn't cooked to suit him. He slapped her across the face! Humiliated, she left the room and he sat back down to finish eating. Somehow I miraculously kept myself from boiling over.

That night I went to his room and said, "I want to tell you something right now. We're friends. I love you, I respect you. But if you ever hit another person in front of me that can not fight back I'm going to tear you apart." We both knew I meant every word.

The next morning I left the chaplain school campus and haven't been back since.

I was heartsick at the thought that I had such a passion for Africa and was now at a complete dead end. A day or two later, on the way to the airport, I said, "God, I guess this means I can't come back to Africa again."

But God answered, *No, this means I'm taking you to a new land in Africa to serve me.* I'd have to develop my own contacts and resources in Africa from scratch. In the middle of a war zone.

Land mines. Roadblocks. Civil war. What exactly was going on in Sudan and Uganda? That whole story would take a book of its own. But in order to fully understand the scope of the miracle that's taken place with our children's ministry, you need to know a little bit about the big picture.

Sudan, in the northeastern part of Africa, is the biggest

country on the continent, three and a half times the size of
Texas. It used to be part of Egypt, which used to be part of
the British Empire. In 1955 a civil war started; in 1956 Sudan
became an independent republic; and less than three years
later, the commander-in-chief of the Sudanese army took
control of the country, outlawed political parties, and tried
to bring all of Sudan under Islamic religious law and the
Arabic language.

The north, where most of the people and power were,
was heavily Islamic and Arabic, but in the south all the education had been provided for generations by Christian
missionaries. People in the south were overwhelmingly
non-Arabic and non-Muslim. While many of them were
Christians, many others just wanted the freedom to worship
and live as they pleased. The northern government, head-
quartered in the capital city of Khartoum, said that if you
were Sudanese, you were an Islamic Arab. End of discussion.

Finally in 1972 the conflict ended with the Addis Ababa
Agreement and a promise of autonomy for the south. An
uneasy peace held until a new hard-line Muslim group
took power in 1983 and basically nullified the Addis Ababa
Agreement, reclaiming control over Southern Sudan. That's
when Colonel John Garang revolted against the northern
government and formed the Sudanese People's Liberation
Army.

In 1989 Lieutenant General Omar al-Bashir seized
power. His Revolutionary Command Council imprisoned
political opponents, outlawed political parties and trade
unions, and zeroed in on crushing resistance to Islam in the
south. Over the next decade the country came unglued bit

by bit. The civil war caused food shortage and unimaginable suffering for the people in the countryside. When the RCC realized they would never defeat the SPLA, they turned loose a radical Muslim militia called the *mujahedeen*. People were murdered by the thousands, many more displaced, and the government refused to let humanitarian agencies in with food and medicine.

As bad as all that was, it wasn't the worst thing the Southern Sudanese people had to deal with. In my opinion the worst menace to the people there is a wild dog named Joseph Kony, who heads a rebel group called the Lord's Resistance Army. These are the maniacs who have devastated Southern Sudan and neighboring Uganda, which is where the LRA originally started and has its base of operations. The fighting goes on along both sides of the border.

Like Sudan in 1956, Uganda gained its independence from the British Empire six years later, then fell apart due to tribal warfare and a poor economy. Southern Uganda had most of the nation's people and wealth. It's where the capital city, Kampala—the center of most of the tourist trade—is located. The northern Ugandans, including many members of the Acholi tribe, felt neglected and shut out by the government of Yoweri Museveni. Like the majority of Ugandans, Museveni is a Christian, though he did come to power in a military coup. (And while the Uganda–Sudan border is a lawless place, Uganda has a much more successful and responsible government than Sudan.)

Joseph Kony formed the LRA from what was left of a rebel group first set up by Alice Lakwena to demand rights for the Acholi people. Some versions of the story say Alice claimed to be demon possessed. In 1987, about a year after she got the resistance movement going, Kony took it over. Since then, the objectives of the LRA have gotten blurred, and these days nobody really knows what Kony and the LRA are fighting for. They don't seem to have any goal or objective other than terrifying people and practicing their gut-wrenching brand of mutilation and disfigurement.

Joseph Kony didn't have much money to pay and maintain his army, so around 1994, about the same time he moved the LRA base of operations from Uganda to Sudan, he started kidnapping children and turning them into soldiers. They're weak, compliant, easy to train, and easy to brainwash. And most soldiers on the other side are going to hesitate before shooting at a child, giving the child a chance to shoot first. In time more than thirty thousand kidnap victims became child soldiers. In 2002 Kony moved his headquarters back to Uganda.

Joseph Kony cultivates a personal mystique. For years every image of him showed him in a fatigue uniform with long beaded dreadlocks and big mirrored sunglasses. He thinks he's on some holy mission. But I'm here to tell you that if anybody on this earth is more evil than Kony, I've never heard of him.

Kony and his men raid villages looking for children to capture. They shock and traumatize the kids as soon as possible to frighten them into doing anything they're told. They sometimes kill their parents in front of them, hacking them to death with machetes or burning them alive. They slice babies out of their mothers' bellies and set them on fire. They make the mother watch before raping and killing her. They cut off noses, breasts, ears, lips, or hands, sometimes forcing children to eat the cut-off pieces.

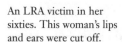

An LRA victim in her sixties. This woman's lips and ears were cut off.

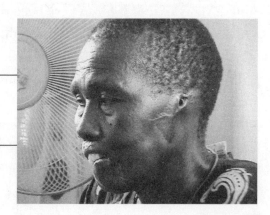

They hand an eleven-year-old boy a machete and order him to disembowel his mother. He does it.

They run off with children from teenagers to toddlers who will become armed soldiers trained to kill children like themselves, to shoot girls on their way to the well or the river for drinking water, to murder parents on command. The soldiers may kill and cut up one or two of their young captives or nail them alive to a tree, as a warning to the others. The ones remaining quickly learn to kill without feeling or remorse. Even some of the youngest will soon carry machine guns almost as big as they are. Others become pack animals, carrying ammunition and supplies for troops on the march. Some become cooks or orderlies. Many, if not most of them, serve as sex slaves. Senior officers get their pick of the older girls; lower ranks get the younger ones; everybody else gets the boys.

The Uganda People's Defence Force gives children and their families in the area some protection, but no one outside the cities in northern Uganda or Southern Sudan feels safe at night. Many of the children have been orphaned by AIDS. Others have had parents killed in the fighting. Even boys and girls who still have their families are targets for LRA raids. Villagers are powerless against the guns and the mindless intensity of the rebels. Many of these fighters were themselves kidnapped as children and remember nothing but a lifetime of killing on Kony's orders. They don't know why they kill; they only know that if they don't, they'll have their own lips chopped off or be decapitated as a lesson to their fellow soldiers.

Because the nights bring the threat of invasion and terror to the villages, thousands of children in northern Uganda have become night commuters, leaving the nightmare of capture behind for the safety of the city. Every afternoon after school they walk—some with bedrolls balanced on their heads and many more with no belongings at all—to the nearest town where they jam into schools, churches, hospitals, anywhere with room on the floor to sleep. Those who have food or money to buy something share with those who don't, though plenty of them will still go to sleep without anything in their stomachs. They trade hunger for a long walk and a night spent on a cold floor. It's the only way they can be sure to be safe from Kony's raids in the countryside.

The heat of the day gives way to the evening breeze as the children come into town. You hear them first, shouting at friends and calling out to their brothers and sisters to stay together. Then you see them, a swirling tangle of brightly colored clothes bobbing through the darkening streets. Some are dressed in little more than rags, but they're bright against the scarred, once-painted wooden doors that open to admit them to a hospital courtyard or schoolroom.

Children being children everywhere, the air is full of laughter, and playmates dart after each other until the room gets too full to run. Wide smiles and sparkling eyes show little hint of fear. They're safe for another night. As routine as it is, every evening is an adventure and every night is fun. There are no adults present, no chaperones or monitors. The children take care of each other.

One small but confident voice starts to sing, clear and silvery in the night. In English with a lilting African accent:

> Never stand away from God,
> Never stand away—Hallelujah!
> Never stand away from God,
> Never stand away.

Other voices immediately join in—everybody knows the song—and the rich African harmony adapted over the years to the simple Western tune fills the room. There's a leader and a chorus, batting the lyrics back and forth and bouncing them off the walls. The beat is energetic, full of life. Little hands start clapping, some on the downbeat and others on the beat in between. The room grows dark—there's no electricity—and the song goes on into the night. Finally the children settle down to sleep. At first light the next morning, some of them gather their meager bedrolls and start the long walk home to their villages. Others just stay in town, spending the day on the street and scavenging for food, until twilight and the next night's sleep.

When I came back to Africa, I believed the best way I could help the people there, especially the children, was to bring medicine and medical help into places that didn't have any. The governments of Sudan and Uganda weren't assisting these people. CARE and the Red Cross and those kinds of organizations stayed away because they said it was too dangerous. That left nobody. Correction: that left me and God and the great big Land Cruiser I bought with a paper sack full of cash.

I'd been driving the mobile clinic back and forth to Africa for about a year when I found my land outside Nimule, where refugees from LRA attacks were trying to set up their own sort of refugee camp a few miles outside of town. That was when God told me to buy that land and start a center for children there. And so I finished up my mobile clinic operation and started working on the orphanage.

Being in the construction business, I started looking for ways to improve on the design of the *tukuls* that my soldier friend Ben and I were building with the help of some local men. One thing I did was dig the floors down below ground level. When you stepped inside you stepped down sixteen inches. That way if you were asleep at night and somebody started shooting, you'd be lying below the line of fire. Instead of plain mud brick, I started making my *tukuls* out of fired brick and cement, with walls three bricks thick to stop a rifle bullet. Later I replaced the thatched roofs with metal, so that we had basically a brick hut with a metal roof in the shape of a native *tukul*.

One of the best security improvements we made on the property was a chain-link fence. The first fence we had was made of bamboo, the poles jammed right next to each other in a solid wall. This is usually the best kind of fence you can build in the bush, and it's a good, strong fence. The problem is that you can't see through it, so LRA soldiers could come from the riverbank right up to the fence undetected and poke a rifle barrel through it or over the top. One time the LRA killed a person on the compound next to us and tried to raid ours. I was back in Pennsylvania that night and got a phone call from one of our soldiers with the news. I said, "I'll be there in three days."

I was ready to give the LRA a lesson they'd never forget. We sat at night waiting for rebels to sneak up toward us. If you saw anybody coming in the moonlight, you didn't call out a name or say anything; you just shot on sight. I sat outside with my AK in my lap, waiting for them to come back . . . but they didn't. My guess is they knew I was there, and they weren't going to shoot at somebody they knew would shoot back. To this day our compound has never been raided, and no enemy has ever set foot inside.

Cornerstone Television of Pittsburgh started doing documentary segments about our ministry. They recognized the need for better protection and gave us thirty-nine thousand dollars for a new fence. During the day we tore down the bamboo fence and had soldiers slash all the underbrush between our compound and the river so no one could use it for cover. We put up a six-foot chain-link fence with two feet of barbed wire on top all the way around, then added four more strings of barbed wire a foot or so off the ground, eight feet from the fence on the outside. The fence had steel poles I designed, with two wheelbarrows full of cement anchoring each pole. At times when the LRA presence was really bad, we had two RPG launchers inside the fence and a PK .30 caliber machine gun in a bunker at each corner. Now that the situation is relatively quiet, ten soldiers still patrol the compound around the clock, but the big hardware is gone. It would take a pretty powerful army to bust through there.

In my travels around Uganda and Sudan, I've been attacked more times than I can count. Sometimes it's when I'm on the offensive, and sometimes it's completely unexpected. Either way I say, "Come on, LRA. I'm ready for you!" They may get me one day, but until then, every time I meet them, my goal is to make their army a little smaller. There's always a chance they can take me out, but if that day ever comes, you can be sure a sizable crowd of them will be going with me.

FIVE

money, missions, and mercenaries

The only thing I fight more often than the LRA is the endless battle for funding. From the beginning, our ministry in Africa has run on a shoestring. But we still have to have money for the shoestring. Compared to the costs in the U.S., most of the things we need—basic food, fuel, clothing, medical supplies, staff salaries—are a fraction of what they are at home. Sometimes, though, scraping together even that fraction seems impossible, no matter how hard we scrimp and budget. The number of children we can save depends on the amount of money we have to work with. If we can't feed a child or give him a bed at night, that's one child facing capture, starvation, and death—one child we can't rescue.

Especially in the early days, we had absolutely no money. We had to improvise, do without, and get very creative to keep things running. Time and again I said, "God, we need money to do this work. You know this better than I do. You know how stressed and stretched we are. You know I have a heart for this ministry and will use my resources responsibly. So help us out here!" But God wouldn't play by my rules. He demanded faith first, then gave our ministry his blessing. He had to see how far I was willing to sacrifice before deciding I was worthy to handle the job.

The first way station between America and our Children's Village in Nimule is the international airport at Entebbe, just outside the capital city of Kampala on Lake Victoria. With 1.5 million people, about the same population as Philadelphia or Phoenix, Kampala is by far the largest city in Uganda. It's a modern city with tall buildings, traffic jams (people drive on the left, a legacy of the British), noise, smoggy air, and busy shops. Although it's directly on the equator, the city is blessedly cool and green thanks to the lake and the four-thousand-foot altitude. The outdoor markets are awash in the brightly colored robes of shoppers looking over piles of fresh tomatoes, potatoes, cucumbers, peppers, and other produce piled on cloths spread out over the pavement.

When we first set up headquarters in Kampala, we had a one-bedroom apartment with bunk beds in the living room. Today the ministry leases a fine guesthouse there—palm trees out front, tile floors throughout, comfortable beds for eighteen people—and earns some income by hosting visitors. Before we had the apartment during those earliest visits, even the cheap hotels were too expensive. I couldn't make my house payment back in Pennsylvania, much less fund a ministry halfway around the world.

In those days I stayed at what looked like a vintage motel on the outskirts of Kampala because it was the cheapest place in town. It was a C-shaped building with a courtyard in the middle, old and threadbare, but always clean. I soon found out that the reason it was so economical is because this "guesthouse" was actually a whorehouse. There was a good-sized sitting room with a TV and stereo, and couches lined the walls all the way around. Four or five girls were always waiting there for men to come in and take their pick. Some of my soldiers and I started having Bible studies in that room. We never preached or pushed or tried to convert anybody. But the customers would come in and see that we were soldiers and then get out of there quickly. The management didn't run us off because they were too afraid of us. Some of the girls started joining us for the Bible study. Over the year or so when I stayed there, several of the girls had a change of heart about their careers, left for more wholesome work, and never came back.

We had the same low budget when it came to meals, so we went from our rooms in the whorehouse to some of the cheapest restaurants in Kampala. I'm talking fish soup and a hunk of maize bread for a dollar. I'm talking places where missionaries would look you in the eye and say, "Don't eat there. You'll die eating in places like that!" But that was all the money I had. I didn't want to eat there, but I ate there without complaining, just like I stayed in the whorehouse without complaining. I believe I was blessed because I stayed and ate in those places. I drove mangy old vehicles most people wouldn't even ride in. I bought used tires and carried four or five old ones on my vehicle's roof because I couldn't afford new ones, and the roads were so bad that tires blew out all the time. I did this, not for a few trips, or a few months, but for years.

In Gulu, between Kampala and the Sudanese border,

where I buy supplies, we went to the cheapest boarding house we could find. Sometimes six of us would sleep in the same room. When I first started coming to Africa, I paid all my own expenses and funded the work I was doing out of my own pocket. But as I spent less and less time running my construction company, my income started melting away. I still had plenty of work, but without me at the job site, projects that should take a week were taking two weeks, so instead of making two thousand dollars on the job, I was making five hundred. Or nothing. Or actually losing money on the deal. On top of that I got cheated by clients who made changes to work orders and then wouldn't pay for them. One deal cost me twelve thousand dollars, and another set me back twenty thousand dollars. I was too busy to argue.

The bills started piling up, and my wife and the rest of my family and friends thought I was crazy to keep going. "If God is in this, why are you so broke?" they wanted to know. "If God is in this, why doesn't he bless you with the resources you need to carry out his plans?" Call it spiritual warfare, call it a test of faith; it was a very hard time in my life that lasted for years. There was a time when I was afraid my marriage was going to be over. I was afraid my wife was going to leave me because she thought I was nuts. I had become fanatical.

In some ways the worst thing of all was the strain it put on our daughter, Paige. My African mission wasn't her vision. All she knew was that her father was spending his time and the family's money on children thousands of miles away instead of on her. She was in danger of losing her home. She was buying her clothes at secondhand thrift shops while her friends were snapping up the latest fashions at the mall. If you were a twelve-year-old girl, would that make any sense to you?

Maybe the worst of the worst was the day she asked me, "Dad, why do you love the African children more than me?" I'm pretty tough, but that punch in the gut was more than I could take. Looking into her wounded eyes as she waited for an answer absolutely tore my heart out. How could I explain it? I could only pray that God would eventually give her wisdom and understanding to know what I was doing and why.

Somehow I pushed on in spite of the financial strain and the burden it put on my wife and daughter. There were times when I thought we'd all go crazy. And yet, even when I was losing everything I had, I would get up behind my pulpit and preach that Jesus is the only way, the only answer, and preach it with a smile. I had to go through the storm with my head held high.

For years the only time any of us got any clothing was when a supply of donated clothes would come in for a shipping container headed for Africa. I hauled a trailer around to the churches that supported us and filled it with clothes. Before we filled the container, we went through the donations, picked out some things we could wear, and kept them for ourselves. During part of that time, I drove a tractor trailer for Feed the Children, a worldwide relief agency based in Oklahoma City. I picked up donated food once a month and delivered it to the food pantries they supplied. I rented the truck and charged the food pantries a delivery fee. My income from that put groceries on our table for almost a year.

If God tells you to do something, before he opens up the door and blesses you with the means to do it, he's going to take you down to nothing. He's going to make sure you have enough faith to be trusted with his work. The low point in my struggle came when we had a crucial need for the ministry and a foreclosure notice on our house at the same time. We had gotten way behind in our mortgage payments because we were sending everything we had to Africa, and I wasn't making money from construction anymore. I had sold my rental property and land, had auctioned off my construction equipment, and was totally dedicated to the children of Sudan.

I'd just come home from Africa and already absorbed one shock. A few weeks earlier, my wife came outside in the morning, and my truck was gone. She reported it stolen to the police, and they called back later in the day and said, "Ma'am, nobody stole your truck; they repossessed it." Now she was telling me to sit down at the kitchen table because we had something to talk about.

She handed me a letter. It was a foreclosure notice. I starting crying and asked, "How much money do we have?"

She said, "Two thousand dollars."

"How much do we need to stop this foreclosure?"

"Two thousand dollars."

How do you look your wife in the eye—your life partner who depends on you and trusts you to support her and keep her safe—and say, "Well, yes, by some great miracle we do have the money to pay the mortgage, but I'm going to send it to our ministry instead, which means we'll soon be out on the street"?

I slammed the notice down on the table and bawled, "They can have the house! Send the money to Africa!" Then she started to cry too. I couldn't stand to watch her, so I walked away.

I sent the money to Africa.

We didn't lose our house. At the last possible minute we scraped up enough money to hold off the foreclosure. And that was when our financial picture started to change. We still have that house in Pennsylvania today, plus the guest-houses in Kampala and Gulu, plus a forty-acre orphanage compound. When I was willing to sacrifice everything I had for Africa, then—and only then—God began showering down blessings on me, my family, and my ministry. Now when I go to Africa, I don't have to eat for a dollar; I can buy the finest meal in town. I drive new vehicles and buy new tires, paid for in cash. When my tires are half worn, I give them to somebody who needs a blessing. I lease one of the finest houses in Kampala, valued at a quarter of a million dollars.

I know there are people who say, "All that guy wants to do is brag about what he has." They're absolutely right! But it's not about what I have or what I have achieved; it's about what God did. I give all the glory to him. When he saw the faith-fulness, then the favor came. The blessings poured down on us to the point where anything we touched began to prosper.

I wish money wasn't such a big deal. It can surely side-track people who are trying to do good works, and it can be a serious distraction that draws attention away from the real focus. It reveals how close to the surface greed and selfishness are, even in the most well-meaning people. And the more institutionalized and bureaucratic an organization is, the more money seems to be a problem, the more waste there is, and the less traction and productive work gets done. Maybe it's not that we need more money donated to charity; we just need to spend it more wisely. In the great scheme of things, our ministry is tiny, with a budget well under a million dollars a year. That still sounds like a lot until you consider that Americans spend six billion dollars a year on potato chips.

Big budgets don't ensure good stewardship or success in delivering aid. Actually, I think you could make a case for the idea that the more money a relief organization has, the less wisely they spend it.

I say this not from reading a report somewhere, but from personal experience. In northern Uganda, one particular NGO has been hauling in food, medicine, and supplies for many, many years. A few years back when the fighting was really bad, the truck drivers working for this organization stopped hauling all supplies because of the ambushes on the road. They wouldn't go into the area where I was working because they were afraid to die. The NGO wouldn't make their truck drivers go in.

This NGO then hired me to haul their supplies for them. That's how we lost our supply truck in 2005. Our driver was speeding through a dangerous area, but once he got to safety he couldn't slow down fast enough and rolled the truck. So we had to get another one. But because of greed, or whatever you want to call it, the organization paid me a fraction of what they were getting paid to deliver their stuff into the hot zone. I did the work for less than it cost me to operate my vehicles. I couldn't even pay for tires out of what I was paid.

An ambushed vehicle

Why would I do this outfit's work for them and then let them hog the lion's share of the money? Because I was there. Unlike some administrator behind a desk somewhere, I had seen the suffering. I lived with these people. I had to watch what happened to people when supplies didn't get through.

What I want to know is why it's easy for a big organization to get millions of dollars through the system, only to end up afraid to deliver the goods, while an organization like mine that is not afraid of war and is willing to go over and beyond to save a life has to struggle so hard with only what we raise ourselves. Untold millions of dollars are misused every year by huge, well-funded organizations that get money from the government.

As hard as it is to figure out why this happens, an even more important question is why the United States trades with and sells military equipment to its enemies. This is international diplomacy at its most insane and most deadly. We trade with countries that are out to undermine us with our own dollars, including Sudan and other radical Islamic countries. People are dying because of it, and I know one man who paid with his life for trying to learn the truth.

In 2000, a man named Steve Snyder with International Christian Concerns (ICC) came to me and said, "Sam, I want you to take me to Sudan and show me everything the U.S. is doing to fuel the war in Southern Sudan." ICC is an organization that spotlights persecution of Christians around the world, including countries that trade heavily with the U.S. I said I would show him what he wanted to see. I took him to the front lines of the Sudanese civil war, just north of the Uganda–Sudan border. There I showed him F-5 rocket launchers with U.S. military serial number plates that had been sold to the Muslim government of Sudan, a government that has been bombing and murdering its own citizens for decades. I took photos of them.

I have no doubt government officials will deny it. They have to. They'll say, "Aw, this man is a liar. He's an uneducated gorilla and he's as bad as the rebels he's been fighting with." But the fact is that the weapons I showed Steve were sold in violation of the Geneva Convention, which says you can't sell weapons to any country in the middle of a war. For the Americans to do what they wanted while still following the letter of the law, the actual transaction and exchange of money took place in Kenya. Steve Snyder found it.

Two months before he died, Steve came to my church and looked me in the face and said, "Sam, I think somebody's going to end up killing me, and I think it's going to be our government."

I laughed and said, "Oh yeah, Steve. Come on!"

He said, "No, I'm serious." Two months later, healthy Steve Snyder died of a rare blood disease under mysterious circumstances.

I'll say it: I believe Steve was killed. He was rattling too many chains in high places. He got a phone call from the White House that literally told him, "Drop it all. Let it go. You don't know what you're getting into." He refused, and soon he was dead.

Greed will lead America down the path to disaster if we don't start thinking about what we're doing. We cannot trade with an Islamic country that leans toward radicalism in any way. We can't sell them our surplus weapons. We can't pretend everything's all right when it isn't. These people hate us. They're out to destroy us. They blew up the marine barracks at the U.S. embassy in Beirut, blew up the USS *Cole* guided-missile destroyer in 2000, blew up the World Trade Center in 2001, and no doubt plan on blowing up other American property and taking American lives. And we're selling (or giving!) them whatever they need to do it with. The radical Muslim world wants to run America; I believe unless we rethink our approach, it's going to end up happening.

We need to spend our money a different way. A few years back, the U.S. government gave three million dollars cash for the care of some refugee camps, which were housing people who Joseph Kony and the LRA displaced. A newspaper interviewed me and asked me what I thought about it.

I said, "I think we got a bunch of stupid people in America. Why do we give three million dollars to feed these displaced people? If you put three million dollars into a refugee camp this month, you'll need another three million next month, and another three million after that. Why don't we just offer three million dollars for Kony's head? You could stop that fight then in no time. It would be a bargain."

As I write this, peace talks have been going on between Joseph Kony and the government of Sudan for more than two years. That's a lot of hotel rooms and breakfast buffets, and America has probably paid for the bulk of it. All to try and deal in a civilized way with a rebel maniac who's a total nutcase. Once in the middle of a meeting of LRA leaders to discuss the peace talks, Kony didn't like what one of his commanders, Vincent Otti, said. What I heard was that Otti recommended that they surrender to the international court and try to negotiate some kind of deal. In response, Kony pulled a pistol and killed him at the table with a shot to the forehead. When people asked later if Kony had really murdered one of his own lieutenants, he said, "No, he's only sleeping." This became a big inside joke. And we're talking peace with someone like that? Every day we waste talking, more people are killed.

Action is the language Kony and Islamic radicals understand, and the more we speak it, the better. It never has bothered me being accused of being a mercenary, even though I'm not. The story got started when a few people in northern

Uganda and a few groups in Southern Sudan didn't like what I was doing and started spreading that rumor. But one group that was bad-mouthing me—I won't mention the name—was ambushed along the road one day, and they sure loved it when my soldiers and I came along and escorted them safely into Gulu. I was the savior that day. Suddenly I wasn't this terrible mercenary after all.

There were stories that I used donations from Christians to buy guns and ammo. I have never bought a single weapon in Africa—machine gun, any kind of gun, grenade, ammunition, you name it—with ministry money or my own money. Every weapon I've ever had was given to me by African governments to protect the people around me, protect the children I've rescued, and protect and rebuild their country.

A lot of people said things about me in the past, but when the bullets are flying and their rear ends are on the line, they have a radically different perspective. If you go to Gulu and start asking questions about me to some of the Red Cross, World Vision, and other aid workers, some will say ugly things. But most of them will say, "Yeah, some people call him a mercenary, but that guy's been here for years, and he'll go in and fight!"

I'll fight anywhere, any time, and I have a dedicated group of SPLA soldiers who put their lives on the line for me every day.

One who's been with me since the beginning is named Nineteen. Others who started out with our ministry left soldering to take higher positions in the provisional government of Southern Sudan when it was formed in 2005. Nineteen was one who said, "No, my higher-up position is with the pastor." He sticks with me.

Deng has also been with me a long time. My favorite story about him happened the first time he ever went on a trip with me. He was on the roof of the car with his AK, and we were ambushed. When I stopped the vehicle to grab my weapon, Deng did a Rambo jump off the roof onto the hood, firing like crazy, and put a big dent in my hood.

I was thinking, *You dirty rotten thing. You just dented up my hood!* He was trying to save my life, and I was worried about my hood. Deng became a very good friend, and today he handles all the money that comes through our missions.

I've already mentioned Peter, one of my bodyguards. When Lynn and Paige came to Africa in 2001, General Michael Majock of the SPLA brought Peter over to our compound and said, "I'm going to give you Peter to guard your family."

I said, "Okay, thank you."

He explained, "Peter is a Dinka warrior, trained from seven years old to be a bodyguard." After a couple of weeks I was heading back to America with my family and took Peter back to his compound.

General Majock said, "Ah, Peter is yours."

And I said, "I know, and I thank you very much. You were a lot of help. My wife really appreciated it."

He said, "But he's yours!"

I said, "Thank you, but we're leaving now." I figured the general didn't understand my English.

Then he said, "No, I *gave* him to you." Of course I know one man cannot "belong" to another, but I appreciated Peter being assigned to provide protection for me and my family. He stayed by my side for several years. Peter is now one of the head of customs coming through the border of Nimele and still works with our ministry.

UPDF soldiers provided to Sam for protection, 2007

Until they came to work for me, most of the men who help us had never seen a city before, never seen electric lights. They had come to serve me, but at the same time were getting educated for jobs in the new government, an opportunity that would otherwise be unavailable to them. During their first trip into Gulu, I took each of them to a buffet at a five-star hotel. Imagine being in the bush all your life, where you only eat enough to survive (never enough to be satisfied), and suddenly finding yourself in front of tables and tables of food offering all you can eat. Watching them chow down is one of the greatest things in the world.

Marco is my head of security at the orphanage, and he is one tall, dark, scary-looking Dinka. Marco's a killer. When he and I took his first trip to the buffet, he was sprawled out at the table, eating like a caveman. His plate was almost empty except for a bite or two of chicken, and the waitress came over to clear it. When she reached for his plate, he grabbed her arm and gave her a seriously nasty look.

Marco, the head of security, in front of one of the machine gun bunkers that protect the orphanage at night

In Arabic he said, "She's trying to take my chicken!" We all started howling with laughter.

"Marco," I said, "she just wants to take your plate for you." He was confused.

"This lady's trying to take my chicken! Why?" It's funny now, but at the time I was afraid our poor waitress was going to get shot for poaching.

One day I was walking through the orphanage compound and saw Marco on the side of the building where the guards sleep, sitting on a little log with one of the children. He was throwing the child in the air, laughing and gooing and gawing at this little child who was laughing as hard as he was. As soon as he caught me looking, Marco put the child down and got a stern expression on his face. He had to look serious for the *mzunga*.

And that brings us back to the children, which is what my story is all about, and a brother and sister named Walter and Angela.

The first thing you notice about Walter is a smile that lights up the sky. The next thing you notice, when he stands still long enough, is the crater in his face where his right eye should be. Imagining his smile is one of the inspirations that keeps me going when the road seems so long and hard. In 2004 Walter and his sister Angela were on the Kitgum Road, traveling from Gulu to Kitgum with their family and some others. Angela was about fifteen at the time, and Walter was five or six. They were an upper-class African family. The parents were merchants who worked the markets, and their father was taking them all to Kitgum in the car.

A group of LRA ambushed them along the road. Following their usual procedure, they went for the driver first, killing the father almost instantly. (That's why for years I drove a vehicle with American left-hand drive. Since cars here are usually right-hand drive, from the outside it looks like I'm the passenger.) The mother was killed quickly with a few machine gun bursts, as were a couple of people riding in the back. Then the soldiers captured Walter, Angela, and their sister, who was about thirteen or fourteen years old. They raped the sister in front of Walter and Angela, beat her, then set her on fire and watched her burn.

While the soldiers were busy tormenting their dying victim, Angela saw a chance to escape. She quickly picked Walter up and started running down the road. The soldiers opened fire on the two small targets with their AKs, dropping them both in a burst of automatic fire. Leaving the body of the sister in flames on the side of the road, they walked up to the fallen figures. One of the armed men nudged them with a scuffed, dusty boot. No response. The soldiers left them for dead and melted back into the bush.

Hours later my SPLA team came upon the grisly scene. Bloody bodies were scattered around the car, and the charred body of the sister still smoldered, giving off the stomach-churning smell of burning flesh. Movement a few yards up the road caught the team's attention. Two little figures writhed in the grass just off the roadway. Somebody had survived the massacre. Running up, the soldiers discovered two children miraculously still alive. Walter had been shot in the eye; Angela had been shot in the neck.

The troops kneeled down in the dirt, gingerly gathered Walter and Angela up in their arms, and sped to the hospital in Gulu as fast as they could. Walter's eye was completely shot out, and bullet fragments were scattered under the skin all over his head and face. Angela had severe nerve damage that paralyzed one whole side of her body. The doctors in Gulu did what they could, and when the two children got out of the hospital they went directly to my home in Gulu. Angela was like a stroke patient, slowly recovering feeling and movement. If she'd had world-class medical treatment when she was first shot, she probably would be a lot better than she is now.

Eventually, in 2006, both of them came to America for treatment. Angela had electric stimulation treatments on her muscles that dramatically improved her ability to move. The treatment involved placing long needles into her muscles and zapping them with electricity. She recovered amazingly well and can walk with confidence. Walter visited America a second time in 2007 for surgery on a tumor that had grown in his eye socket. At first the doctor thought that a single bullet went through Angela's neck and hit Walter in the face. But they told me after the surgery that they think Walter was hit with his own bullet. His face is still full of bullet fragments. You can actually feel one of them under the skin on his head.

For every story like this that ends on a positive note, there are countless others we'll never know about—children who are victims of terrible crimes where God is the only witness. I have a special connection with those tender, innocent hearts; I feel a special calling to save and protect kids, because there was a time when I preyed on them as heartlessly as any LRA soldier. I wasn't out to shoot them, but in a way I was even more dangerous. I represented fun and excitement, only to lure them in to satisfy my own desires.

My heart aches for girls like Angela. Part of it is the compassion I think any father would have for a defenseless girl who has been so brutally abused. Looking into Angela's face, I can't help seeing the face of someone else. Someone who suffered so much on account of me. Someone whose memory inspires me to help children when I think I have nothing left to give. Someone God sent to teach me dark truths about myself—hard lessons that prepared me for my life's work in a way I could never have imagined.

SIX
in the wilderness

Her name was Jackie. I met her in 1976 when I was fifteen. She had long, blond hair; fair skin; sparkling blue eyes; and a big, bright smile that lit up her whole face. Jackie was a beautiful girl looking for excitement. She was way too young to realize it, but she was also looking for a boy who would love and protect her. Something tricked her into thinking that boy was me.

I had already been sleeping with girls and older women for about two years when I convinced Jackie to sleep with me. It didn't take a lot of convincing because I already had a reputation in town, and she wanted the experience. It was her first time, and she worshipped me. She would do anything I asked her to do with me or anybody else because she loved me and wanted to please me.

In spite of that, I used her as I did every other female during those wild years. Drugs, sex, and money were my gods, and I bowed down to them with gusto. I took advantage of Jackie. I gave her the first hit of drugs she ever had and got her messed up on narcotics. I taught her that her life was no good. I showed her that she was not special. She was not a jewel. A young woman has that special gift of her purity, and she should be encouraged to save that precious gift for the person she wants to spend the rest of her life with. I stole that gift from her and thought nothing of it. It was just another trophy, another conquest.

Jackie had an abortion. She didn't know who the father was, but a lot of people said the child was mine. I feel in my heart that they were right. It was all over before I knew anything about it. I wonder what I would have done if I had known. We all should feel the same when it comes to abortion: it's killing a human being. But at a time when you're fully possessed and living for the devil, you don't care.

Jackie was the one I've felt most guilty about, but she wasn't the only young girl whose purity I stole. There were four others at least. It just didn't matter to me. All that mattered was the party.

One night three other guys and I had taken turns with this one girl, and the party was winding down when an acquaintance named Donny dropped by. Donny was one of the best-known drug dealers in town, and he decided he wanted a little session with this girl too. She turned him down and started walking home. Donny followed her in his car, picked her up, beat her, and raped her. She reported him to the police, and the other guys at the party and I had to give sworn affidavits about what happened. Because she had been with so many other partners that evening, they couldn't charge Donny with rape so he got away with it. The girl's stepfather said he was going to kill Donny for what he did. It was years before I found out how that story ended. Donny eventually ended up dead under mysterious circumstances. It wouldn't surprise me if the stepfather had made good on his threat.

By that time I'd dropped out of high school. I had moved out of the house when I was sixteen to make it easier to party, and quit school in the eleventh grade. Sometime around then I started carrying a sawed-off shotgun. I never killed anybody with it, but soon I had a reputation as a bad dude who always had a sawed-off within reach. It was a reputation I gladly encouraged. My friends and I started going back and forth to Florida looking for fun. That was when we went from just using drugs to dealing drugs and, most profitable of all, robbing drug dealers. The dealers always had plenty of cash, and they sure weren't going to report us to the police. Because I carried a gun everywhere, bar fights turned into knife fights, which turned into gunfights. I always had either a .25 automatic, a .380 automatic, or a .38 Special with me, and carried a .38 derringer as a spare.

The first time I ever went to Florida for the summer, I went with my high school buddy Joe Ramonovitch. He was better looking than I was—short, blond hair; long face; high cheekbones; a scraggly beard like all of us tried to grow— but I was a much better shot.

We spent six days partying our way from Minnesota to Orlando and found a place to stay in a Lockhart, Florida, trailer park. My brother George lived nearby and told us about this place. We rented a twelve-by-sixty-foot trailer that sported a peeling coat of off-white paint and a little rickety porch at the front door. There were trees around us, but lawn grass was scarce, and any sign of shrubs or flowers was nonexistent. There were no paved roads or parking lots, just sand everywhere that we constantly tracked inside, creating a layer of grit over everything. For company we had rats and cockroaches galore, but we didn't care. It was a place where we could drink and shoot up any time, and that's all we worried about. Later we moved to another trailer that was a bit of an improvement, with more windows and bright yellow trim. But as we had in the other place, we still parked our motorcycles in the living room.

Trailer parks like these were their own little worlds. They were full of alcohol and drugs, especially crack cocaine, even though that wasn't really popular back then. Cocaine and heroin were what most of the residents used. It was a community of outlaws, and we were model citizens.

Daytona was just a few miles up the road on the Atlantic Coast, and it was one rockin' kind of place. There was plenty of action in the bars in the historic area, where the streets were narrow and the old buildings stood close together. There was even more going on at the beach, where the restaurants and bars spilled right down to the water; you could still drive on the sand, which was a famous tradition there.

My life in Florida during those years was one unending fight. One of the first and biggest was after a drug deal went sour, and we went to visit our trading partners at their trailer. I announced our arrival by busting their door in with a baseball bat. Inside we had a free-for-all that sent me to the hospital for forty stitches in my head where somebody whacked me with a tire iron. The police came and arrested us all. Fortunately the other guys were the ones who had the drugs. They were also illegal aliens from Canada. That—plus the fact that I was underage—got me off with the sheriff's department when I could have gotten ten years.

There was a pier on the Daytona boardwalk where small-

time drug dealers used to meet. It was a great place to rob
them. One time two friends and I robbed a couple of dealers of about half a pound of marijuana and one hundred hits
of LSD. We drove up and down the beach yelling, "Pot!" or
"Acid!" depending on the type of person we saw. After a
couple of sales, two young guys came up to buy from us. The
first one pulled out a .38 Special and pointed it at my head.
Turnabout is fair play, I thought. We'd stolen the stuff and
now somebody was stealing it from us. But then the second
guy pulled out a gun and a badge. We weren't being robbed;
we were being arrested.

I had a long beard, long hair, and a fake ID saying I was
twenty-one, but I was only seventeen. Once I knew they
wouldn't arrest me (I was underage and they didn't want to
go through the hassle), I started trash-talking them. They
handcuffed my hands in front, shackled my feet, chained my
hands to my feet, and shuffled me off to the juvenile deten-
tion facility. It was like walking into middle school—nothing
but kids! In a few hours, my brother George bailed me out,
and we got my friends Joe and Pat out. As soon as Joe was
bailed, he and I headed back to Minnesota.

But Florida kept calling us. A few months later we were
back, and before long bar fighting turned into a regular after-
work hobby. One night after some serious whiskey drinking,
four other guys, one woman, and I decided to take on the
whole crowd at the ABC Liquor Lounge outside Apopka.
Too bad we didn't notice ahead of time that everybody but us
had on pointy-toed cowboy boots. It was not a good place for
a bunch of bikers to start a fight, but by the time we figured
that out, the bottles were already flying. When we tried to

escape through the front door, we found a cluster of unhappy rednecks blocking our way.

We headed for the back door, but there was a huge guy there who was wider than the doorway. I hit him three or four times, but he didn't flinch. I got out my pocketknife and started carving up his forehead. He went down, and I headed for the door again when—*crash!*—I took a beer bottle to the forehead, mistakenly (I hope) from the woman who was with us. Bleeding like a stuck pig, I bolted for the door with the rest of my bunch, but now the bouncer blocked our exit. I had thought about using my gun before but hadn't. Now I put my pistol to the bouncer's throat. Neither of us said a word, but he moved out of the way and let us by.

I was the last one to the car. Sprinting across the back parking lot, I heard a gunshot and saw a man firing at me from behind a truck. Just then the bouncer came running at me for more. I knocked him down and returned fire toward the truck. I dove through the window as our car sped off. As soon as we made it to the highway, we saw a roadblock—two police cruisers across the road with their red lights flashing. I grabbed a shotgun off the backseat, leaned out the window, and fired forward. The cops scattered, and we flew around the roadblock.

Screaming down the two-lane road, we tried to put some distance between us and the ABC Liquor Lounge. Then we saw a sea of red lights in the distance. But this time instead of two police cars, there were eight. A powerful floodlight locked on us from above, and I heard the chopper overhead. We were sunk. I handed the shotgun to a buddy who jammed it down behind the backseat.

The police swarmed over the car, dragged us out, hand-cuffed us, and searched our car for the shotgun. They couldn't find it. Later they took the seat out, and it still wasn't to be found. Somebody was looking out for me: committing a crime with a gun carried a five-year minimum prison term. Because I was seventeen and wouldn't get in as much trouble, I took the fall for everybody. I ended up in jail at first because of my fake ID. After about five days, George came and bailed me out again. He didn't have any money, so he put up his motorcycle—a 1947 Panhead Harley, black and chrome—as collateral. A couple of weeks later, the charges were dropped (to the bail bondsman's disappointment), and George went back and claimed his bike.

It turned out that there was some sort of clerical error, and the charges had been reduced but not dropped. I moved back to Minnesota, and when I didn't show up for court, a warrant was issued for my arrest. It was never served.

I thought I'd end up dead or back in prison if I stayed in Florida, but Minnesota was pretty rough too this time around. As usual when trouble came along, I didn't run from it; I ran to meet it halfway.

One November night a friend was taking me home from a late party. Driving down a dark, deserted highway, we stopped and picked up someone walking along with his thumb out. I thought, *This guy's lucky to get a ride out here this time of night.* He climbed in the back, and as we started up again he said, "Take me to Bena," which is a little town up the road. I was almost passed out in the front, but I heard my friend say, "I'm not going to Bena. I'm only going to Cohasset."

The news didn't sit too well with our passenger. In an eyeblink he pulled out a knife, lunged up from the backseat, and held the blade against my friend's neck. Messed up as I was, I noticed that move out of the corner of my droopy red eye. "No," the rider snapped, "take me to Bena."

I was not going to take any stuff from this guy. I reached my foot over the floor hump, put it on top of my friend's foot and floored it. We started flying down the narrow highway. My friend tried desperately to yank his foot off the gas but I was mashing down with all my weight. He and the hitchhiker were both screaming, "Stop! Stop! Pick up your foot!" I screamed at the guy in the backseat, "Go ahead, stab him. Stab him. We'll all die tonight!"

The hitchhiker started freaking out. He lowered the knife and said, "Let me out! Just let me out!" As soon as he took the knife away from my friend's neck, I jumped into the backseat and started fighting him. I got hold of his knife and twisted it out of his hand. We kept going at it, and finally I stabbed him with his own knife. My friend turned off onto an old country road. As I threw the hitchhiker out of the car, he tried to grab my foot, so I kicked him a couple of times in the face. He quit moving, and I didn't know at the time whether I'd killed him or not. I got back in the car, and my friend tore off toward the highway. The backseat was covered with blood. I found out later that the guy made it all right. I guess that night convinced my friend I was too wild for him; I've never seen him since.

My life was starting to get out of hand to the point where even I couldn't handle it. Since I had moved back from Florida, I'd been sharing a house with a couple of other friends, a little cracker box of a house with a few steps up to the stoop and a couple of pairs of windows across the front. Later I moved to an apartment with my friend Delane Watson. On Friday and Saturday nights, Delane and I sold fifty to a hundred dime bags—ten dollars' worth—of cocaine out of that place. Delane was several years older than I was, with shaggy brown hair and a full mustache. I was eighteen by then but still looked older than I was. I had a mustache too, the standard scraggly beard, and a sort of brown afro hairdo. If it had been straight, it would have hung down my back, but it was curly and kind of frizzed up. I thought it made me look cool, and the girls loved it. Those curls framed a face that was usually frozen in a self-satisfied smirk. And while I may not have been as tall as some of the other guys, I was all muscle.

For a couple of months I moved from the apartment to a house on a farm, where I knew a man who would eventually get arrested for big-time drug dealing while I was living there. When he heard the police were coming and didn't have time to escape, he gave me a half pound of hashish. His bail was so high that he couldn't afford to get out of jail. I figured this was a good time for a change of scenery. I had been going back and forth to Florida for years and decided to move there for good.

This time in Florida I had the first steady, decent-paying, legal job of my life, thanks to two hard-working people named Mr. and Mrs. Oliver. They were the first responsible adults who treated me with anything close to respect. They knew nothing about my private life before I got to Florida, and it was their style to give everybody the benefit of the doubt. They bought oranges on the tree, hired people to pick them, then sold the fruit and paid the tree owners and pickers. My brother George was already working for them, and I joined him after I moved. George and I got responsible jobs—we were field foremen who handed out ladders in the orange groves and organized the pickers into lines.

I'd been around trouble long enough to see it coming, and some of the pickers we worked with were troublemakers who needed supervision. The Olivers paid their workers in cash and brought as much as eight thousand dollars into the field some days, so I stood close by with a gun or a club on payday to make sure everything went smoothly. I whittled a club about three inches thick from an orange branch with a grain running so it wouldn't break. Kind of a *Walking Tall* stick. I carried it until Mr. Oliver asked me to get rid of it because he was afraid I was going to kill somebody.

Before I handed it over to Mr. Oliver, that stick got plenty of use, although sometimes I took a more creative approach to dealing with troublemakers. Some of the Haitian pickers were big into voodoo and would put a so-called hex on me or the Olivers or anybody else who tried to keep them in line. One day—back when I was doing drugs every day—a big snake came crawling through the orchard. I chased it down, grabbed it by the tail and head, looked at the Haitians, and said, "Watch this!" Then I bit its head off. After that, not only did the Haitians leave me alone, they wouldn't even look at me. And they never tried that voodoo hooey around me again.

The Olivers made good money and paid us well. I looked out for them, and they took care of me, including bailing me out of jail. They always seemed willing to give me another chance, which was the way they treated everybody. I didn't allow anyone to make fun of them, or make fun of me being with them because they were black and I was white. Some whites warned me that residents there killed white people, and I knew of whites who came to buy drugs and wouldn't get out of the car. Though no other white people lived in the neighborhood, I moved into a trailer in the Olivers' backyard. They invited George and me to their Christmas parties and other family events as though we were their children. They were second parents to me. They were the first people who ever gave me a sense of self-respect, and the first to show by their own example that what matters in life has nothing to do with the color of your skin and everything to do with the compassion and commitment in your heart. I wish I could introduce the Olivers to every American and every African who has ever let race or tribe dictate how they feel about anybody.

Over the years I had completely adopted the biker lifestyle, and I had the leather, the chain wallet, the beard, and the tattoos to prove it. I made my own tattoos using toilet paper ashes and a needle, the way they do it in jail. I loved riding bikes, hanging with bikers, and giving out my opinion free of charge to all comers about anything to do with the biking world. Like every other bunch of guys who share a common interest, bikers have road trips, meets, rallies, races, and other events so they can get together and talk shop. One of the best biker events in the country was just up the interstate from us.

Bike Week in Daytona Beach was one of the highlights of

the year for my buddies and me. What started back in the 1930s as a motorcycle race on the beach had morphed into a ten-day invasion of bikers from all over the U.S. and beyond. Daytona's palm-lined streets were choked with hundreds of thousands of motorcyclists looking for a good time. In every direction there was row after row of bikes loaded with chrome and covered with incredible paint jobs: flames, skulls, girls, every kind of design imaginable airbrushed or painted on. A lot of the customized bikes sported tail fins, sidecars, roofs, and anything else a designer could dream up and weld together.

Of course where there are bikes and bikers there are biker chicks. They were in Daytona by the thousands, dressed to highlight their assets—one of the most popular outfits being leather chaps over a bikini. The scene was awash in drinking and drugs. Just the place for young Sam Childers to go in March 1981.

I was headed there in a van cruising up I-4 in Florida doing some pretty heavy partying, when a guy I knew pulled up alongside us on his chopper and hollered over that he wanted to buy some drugs. To do the deal, we pulled off at a roadside rest area with some picnic tables and trees. He and the girl riding behind him got off the bike and got in the van. I didn't really notice her that much at the time. As per usual, we all shared some of the drugs so the guy could make sure the merchandise was as advertised. I saw the two of them a few more times during Bike Week, but didn't think anything of it.

A couple of weeks later I got hired as shotgunner on a drug deal. It was my job to carry a gun to the transaction and be ready to use it at the first sign of trouble. I wore a 9-millimeter pistol into the bar and carried a 12-gauge shotgun in a duffel bag for backup. The place was called the Fox Hole and it looked like any of a thousand grimy strip bars in Florida. Colored lights blinked around beer signs, turning the pitch black into frenetic images flickering through stale cigarette smoke onto dingy tables splotched in last night's beer, scattered between well-worn plastic booths. As I sat down where I could keep an eye on the action, a waitress came up. I didn't want to be distracted and waved her off, but she said, "Don't you remember me? I sure remember you."

It was the girl riding with my buddy who'd stopped us to buy drugs a couple of weeks before. Her name was Lynn.

"I can't talk now," I said. "I'm busy." To reassure myself I felt for the cold steel of the 12-gauge through the rough canvas of the duffle.

"You really don't remember me?" She was persistent, I had to give her that. But I had work to do, and if my boss looked over and saw me talking to a waitress instead of keeping my eye on business, I was gonna be in big trouble. I was supposed to stay alert for when the buyer and seller walked in; I needed to shake this girl, but I had to do it in a way that wouldn't attract attention or look suspicious.

"Okay, okay," I said. "Give me your number, and I'll call you tomorrow." She scribbled her phone number down for me and finally got out of my hair. She went back to work, and so did I.

The next day I called her.

We fell in love real fast, and it wasn't long before we were living together, moving around from place to place, landing wherever we could live really cheap, selling drugs to pay the rent. We never seemed to have enough money even for the basics, like food. There was one time when we were out of money and hadn't had anything to eat for two or three days; we were staying in the hotel room where we lived in Apopka. For the first time in my whole life, I felt responsible for somebody; it was Lynn, and she was hungry.

There was a park not far from our hotel with a pond that always had ducks in it. I had some change in my pockets and a few rounds of ammunition. I went to the pond, shot a duck with a .38 pistol, and brought it home for us to eat. I also bought a loaf of bread and a dozen eggs with the change I had, and I told Lynn, "If you stick it out with me, I promise you will never go hungry again."

We decided to move to Georgia and try to get a fresh start; we landed in Jesup, where I had done some roofing work. Right away I started selling drugs again. Marijuana. I'd go back and forth to Orlando every couple of weeks for half a pound at a time. We had an old car Lynn's father gave us that we never titled. I just stole a different license plate every week, and we ran our drugs in that.

One good thing that happened in Jesup was that I met somebody else who had faith in me and treated me better than I deserved. Lynn's uncle Larry had an auction house and paid me fifty dollars a week to come once a week and work for him there. He also let me sell used tools he had. I filled up our old car with them and sold them on the road. It made me feel good that he trusted me to go out and do that.

After about three months, when we wanted to go back to Florida and needed money for the trip, we sold our car to a fortune-teller. She wanted to trade the car for telling my fortune, but I wouldn't even go in her house. Lynn and I took a Greyhound bus to Orlando and found a place to live at Mudd's Trailer Park. And that's what it was—mud, mud, mud! It was one of the filthiest places I've ever seen. I started doing roofing work, still selling drugs on the side, and Lynn got a job packing carrots. Even so, our pockets were usually empty because we spent every cent we earned on drugs.

One day Lynn was sick with a fever, probably from trying to work days on end without food. I told her I'd go ask my boss for some cash. I had promised Lynn we would never go hungry again, and I was feeling rotten about breaking that promise. I went to my boss and told him I needed twenty dollars right away.

"I don't have it on me, Sam," he said. "But payday's tomorrow. I'll give it to you then." I got a little hot and told him I couldn't come to work tomorrow if I didn't have some money right then.

I decided to hitchhike to Orlando and sell some blood. I could get fifteen dollars for a pint, and then we could eat. I could have asked my parents for money, but I was too proud. I was going to make it on my own. Mom and Dad had moved to Orlando while Lynn and I were living in Jesup. In the middle of what had been hundreds of acres of orange groves, Dad had gotten a job at Walt Disney World building Spaceship Earth—an eighteen-story geodesic globe made out of metal triangles, set in the Epcot part of the park. The huge sphere would house a planned, futuristic city. While much of this type of work went to union laborers, many of the union ironworkers didn't want to work at those heights; but Dad would work doing anything to provide for my mom.

I was walking down the road with my thumb out, and who should come driving along but my mother. Mom pulled alongside me and stuck her head out the window. "The Lord woke me up this morning and told me I should come to your house today," she said. "He even told me to come this way instead of the route I usually take. Why aren't you at work?"

"I'm going to Orlando to give blood because I need to buy some food."

Her eyes flashed with fire. "No, you're not," she said. "Get in this car. I'm taking you to the store to buy groceries." And that's just what she did, though I only let her buy enough necessities to get us by for a few days. She kept putting things in the cart and I kept taking them out. I was only going to accept essentials.

Not long afterward, I met Clyde Carter. I'd been working as a roofer, and Clyde hired my boss to subcontract a job. Clyde was balding, wore wire-rimmed glasses, and lived his life in a wheelchair. He was a respected contractor and a fair boss. He also claimed to be President Jimmy Carter's cousin, but I never found out if he really was or not. One day he stopped by the job site where I was working, had a look around, and said to me, "Things are looking good. I'll come by tomorrow when you're finished and pay you."

I said, "I'll be finished today, and I want to be paid today."

"I don't think so," Clyde said. "There's more to do than you can get done in a day."

"Nope," I said, "I'll be done today." I could tell he thought I was crazy or showing off or didn't know how much work I had left.

"All right. I'll be back at four this afternoon and see how you're doing."

When he got back I was sitting under a tree with the ladder and tools beside me and all the work was done. He paid me and then handed me his card. "If you want to change your life, call me."

What was up with that? I wondered.

The next day I did call him and he invited me to his house in Longwood. It was a nice one-story ranch painted off-white with a little covered porch and a big tree in the front yard branching over most of the house. Clyde met me at the front door in his wheelchair. Instead of inviting me inside, he handed me a twenty-dollar bill. "If you really want to change your life," he said, "take this and go get your hair cut and come back."

Nobody, and I mean nobody, told me what to do with my hair. I had long biker hair, and that's what I wanted. My gut reaction was to say, "Up yours, buddy!" and spend the money at the nearest bar.

But there was something about his honesty that grabbed me. *Why does he care about me? Why does he want me to change my life?* Nobody had ever talked to me like that before. I decided it was worth a shot and went back to my car.

What have I got to lose? I turned the key and headed toward the barbershop. *I'm broke and on drugs*, I figured. *I'm living in a filthy trailer full of rats and roaches. The hair will grow back. Besides, I want to see what's next.*

Getting cleaned up felt weird and good at the same time. As soon as I got back to my car, I went straight back to Clyde's house. This time he invited me in.

"I need some help running my jobs," he said. "I can't get around so good," he continued, gesturing toward his wheelchair, "and somebody like you could be a big help."

"You got a deal," I said. And for the next two or three months I was his legs, his gofer on job sites, running errands and checking on things. Trust grew quickly between us; he had been waiting for the right person to bring into his business, and I enjoyed working with someone who needed and appreciated me.

Clyde trusted and appreciated me so much that he called me in one day and asked if I wanted to be his partner. I couldn't believe it. I was a success! I was so proud. He changed the name of the company to V. M. Carter and Sam Childers Roofing, but his investment in me didn't end with that. He continued to patiently and expertly teach me the ropes of the roofing trade, giving me business pointers that have helped me ever since.

Way more important than any business advice, Clyde taught me that God doesn't make junk.

"God made you in his image," Clyde said, "and he doesn't make mistakes."

Clyde taught me to look at myself from the inside out. He said the important thing is not—as I had been taught—to worry about what other people think, but to look deep within ourselves at who we are in our own minds. He taught me to stop trying to show and tell people who I am, and look deep inside my own heart at what was there. He said what I saw would make me want to change the kind of person I was.

"Don't *tell* the world who you are," he urged. "*Be* who you are, and the world will see it." This didn't all register at once, but he planted seeds in rocky soil that slowly, slowly began to take root.

Along with telling me to get my hair cut and my heart changed, Clyde told me to get married. He didn't think Lynn and I should be living together outside of marriage. By this time, I had decided that Clyde's advice was worth taking. He was not what I would call a religious person, but he was a faithful man and had a genuine selflessness like I had never seen.

So on December 19, 1982, Lynn and I got married in Clyde's living room. I was twenty years old. Lynn had told me once, "I knew I was going to marry you the minute I saw you," and sure enough, she was right. On our wedding day, we moved into a house not far from Clyde's on Land Avenue. It was a simple little ranch house with a porch around one corner and some brown shutters on the windows. No mud. No rats. Lynn and I felt on top of the world.

I kept working hard for Clyde even though I still had a huge appetite for drugs. I was doing a lot of heroin and cocaine and had to shoot up in the morning before work. Seeing Clyde, being part of his business, and getting a taste of the straight life made me realize that as long as I was a slave to drugs I was never going to get far with my life.

Lynn and I needed another fresh start.

In the fall of 1984, we went on a vacation to Central City, Pennsylvania, to visit my parents, who had moved back into the house I grew up in. I knew Lynn was ready for a change too, so while we were there I asked her if she thought she could live there. After a quick look around, she said yes.

We were making plans to move, when my wonderful friend Clyde dropped dead of a heart attack. His business was shut down, but I was blessed to get a lot of the tools and equipment that would be useful for starting a new life in a new place.

I had no idea that my world was about to change so drastically. The move to Central City was another step in a journey that took me places I could never have imagined.

SEVEN

anatomy of a rescue

The adrenaline rush starts before we ever get on the road. Will we find children alive today? Dead? Wounded? How many? Where are their families? Will we flush out any LRA? Kill anybody? Will any of us be killed? Will I die today and miss my daughter's wedding? Lots of questions and no answers.

We check our weapons. One reason AK-47s are so popular is that they're virtually indestructible. Dust and mud and spotty maintenance don't seem to faze them. We check our ammo supply, which is always more than adequate. I travel with plenty of firepower. The vehicles have been inspected to make sure all the maintenance is up-to-date. All that's left to do is move out.

Our African operation has rescued more than nine hundred refugees of all ages. More than half of them were children who had been captured by the Lord's Resistance Army. These youngest victims spend anywhere from a few days to years with the LRA. In some cases the rebel army abandons them, and in others they escape, even though they're brainwashed and usually too scared to try that.

LRA attacks come without reason, without warning.

These rebels have no evident objective beyond killing, maiming, and demoralizing their victims, who are almost always innocent, unarmed villagers, mostly women and children. These twisted followers of Joseph Kony are too chicken to fight soldier against soldier—many of them are poorly trained children themselves—so they prey on the helpless, pitting soldier against child or soldier against woman. Soldiers sweep through the village burning *tukuls*; trampling crops; stealing, scattering, or butchering the animals; killing or disfiguring the adults; and kidnapping the children.

News about a raid comes to me from the locals through the "bush telegraph," a long-established informal communication network that's as fast as any phone and much more accessible. In fact, unless you have a satellite phone, telephone service of any kind is rare in the bush. Nobody wants to install or maintain telephone lines in places where the rebels could attack any minute.

While no two rescues are exactly alike, this particular trip into the bush has a lot in common with previous operations. I got word of an LRA attack on a village along the road to Pageri about twenty miles away, an hour's drive along the rutted dirt road through the bush from Nimule. After so many years of fighting, large numbers of people who used to live in the countryside have moved closer to Nimule for protection or they've picked up stakes and left the area entirely. As you drive east and north along the road, you can see the population gradually thinning out. Close to town there are plenty of people on the road walking or riding bicycles. The farther from town you drive, the fewer people there are.

We snake along through the bush in our Land Cruiser as fast as the rutted, rocky road will allow. As usual, we have a brand-new set of tires, cheap insurance in places where the roads are unpredictable and being stranded could mean dying as sitting ducks awaiting an ambush. The morning is already scorching hot under a cloudless sky when we roll on through the tall grass past an occasional bush or acacia tree, their silhouettes squashed into a horizontal shape, almost like a rectangle of leaves and branches balanced on top of a trunk.

I have my AK bouncing around in its customary position on my lap, the barrel resting on my left arm and poking out the window. My SPLA squad rides in the back, some dressed in fatigues and some in slacks and brightly patterned shirts. None of us talk much. All thoughts are on our destination and what we might find there. As the village comes into view, we strain to see or hear any hint that LRA soldiers might still be around. We don't want to be surprised in case they heard our car coming and are waiting in ambush. Nothing moves anywhere around us; there is no sound, no insects, no animals in the area to make noise. Even the bugs are afraid to stay where the rebels had been. The only sound comes from our little two-truck convoy as we pull within sight of the village.

The low thatched roofs of the *tukuls* and storage sheds pop up into view all of a sudden. We are in the middle of the village before we know it is there. Around us are maybe two dozen *tukuls* dotting the edge of the clearing where the village common had been. Crops are trampled, cattle and chickens scattered. Some of the *tukuls* had their mud brick walls bashed in. Others were burned, leaving the smell of charred thatch and human flesh hanging in the air. Fresh graves, some of them covered with bricks, are scattered through the village near the entrances of the victims' *tukuls*. The LRA killed twenty-seven people in the village that day and wounded many more. They abducted children, of course, some of whose parents were murdered as they watched.

On the road to mile 40, (one of the biggest conflict fighting areas in that part of Southern Sudan) with SPLA, 2000

The locals know who we are and why we are there. A couple of my soldiers go out into the bush to find children who have been scattered in the raid or grabbed by the LRA, then left behind. Some of them, maybe most, will have at least one parent or another relative who could take care of them, though the adults sometimes tried to hide that from us; they figure we will take better care of the children than they can, plus they won't have another mouth to feed. We will sort all that out later.

What we have to do now is wait for word to spread that we are there and for the children to come to us out of the bush or for our SPLA soldiers to find them. I'm not very good at waiting. I sit in the Land Cruiser with the door open, saying a word now and then to one of the soldiers, but mostly keeping quiet. We very seldom ran across rebel soldiers in the bush with the children, which was all right by me. The LRA would just as soon kill their captives as let them go, or a child might be hit by crossfire. We never invade LRA strongholds for the same reasons—our appearance there could end a child's life by murder or collateral damage.

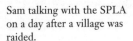

Sam talking with the SPLA on a day after a village was raided.

I hear footsteps rustling in the tall grass and look up to see a woman in a colorful summer dress and a big white necklace. She walks forward with a shy smile, holding a two- or three-year-old child by the hand. The little one has a red patterned shirt and red shorts, looking well fed and healthy. Is he related to the woman? A freshly orphaned refugee? She leads him to the truck and speaks to one of the soldiers. As she talks, another woman, younger and dressed in bright yellow, appears with a baby on her hip. It could be her brother or her son or a baby she found abandoned in the bush. Then three boys walk out of the tall grass, three stair-steps with the oldest one about ten or eleven. Soldiers talk to the adults. Where are the parents? Aunts or uncles? Supposedly these children are all orphans. They tell us there are more hiding out but they're still too afraid to come back to the village. I tell them we'll send a truck back in two days to get anyone else.

We return with the children to the orphanage where Slinky Schillingi, our compound manager, interviews them and fills me in on the details. Slinky had polio as a child and walks in a distinctive way that somehow reminds you of a toy Slinky, pulling his feet around from the side with each step instead of putting one foot straight in front of another. It doesn't slow him down though, doesn't dampen his enthusiasm for doing his work, and surely doesn't keep him from being very much in charge.

According to the survivors he talks to, two children were shot and killed, and five more are still in the bush. The oldest boy we brought back is named Emmanuel. He's very quiet, barely speaks above a whisper, and looks down at the ground. Sometimes he glances up to the side but never looks anyone in the eye. He saw the two children killed. He saw his mother beaten with a rifle butt and both parents shot to death. The blank expression on his face is almost cracked by a quiver of the lip, corners of the mouth turned down, but he holds fast. Doesn't let the emotion out. He can't. Doesn't know how. What he saw is too horrible to think about now. It may come out later in the nightmares so many of these children have.

Another new arrival sports a brand-new *Aristocats* sweat-shirt from our stock of donated clothes. She has precious, delicate features and talks even less than Emmanuel. She is seven years old, and her name is Gift. She doesn't know where her parents are. She spent a month carrying luggage for the LRA. Our caretakers say she was probably sexually assaulted, but she says nothing about it. I tell Slinky to let every child know that they are safe from the soldiers they know as *Tom-Tom*, meaning "cut-cut." Every child deserves to wake up in the morning and not be afraid, to face the future without worrying about whether he or she will see someone killed that day or be killed him- or herself.

—

It's a privilege and a joy to rescue these children and give them a home, but it's even better when we can reunite them with their parents. On another rescue we brought two young teenage boys, Martin and James, back to the orphanage. The LRA had kidnapped them and used them as pack animals to carry supplies. They'd also probably used them for their own debased sexual gratification.

The boys' families had been scattered in the raid, but we were able to locate Martin's parents and get word to them that their son was safe. Along with a few soldiers, I took Martin to a meeting place in the bush on the side of the road and waited for his family. In a few minutes a woman parted the tall grass and stepped into the clearing where we were. She wore a crisp, white blouse and a flowing-bright pink skirt with bold flower designs—happy clothes for a happy reunion. Martin was sitting in the back of the Land Cruiser, and as soon as she saw him she started to run. With a huge smile on her face, she flung open the rear door, reached in, and picked up her son. Long and lanky as he was, his feet almost dragged the ground. She sat down in the dirt with him on her lap and tenderly felt his arms and legs, making sure he was all right. There's no telling what shape his heart or his spirit were in after his experience, but at least physically he seemed okay.

A few minutes later Martin's father joined us, looking like a well-dressed suburbanite in white slacks, white shoes, and a pullover sweater. He spoke to us in English. "Thank you. Thank you very much," he repeated over and over.

In these two instances we found families of at least some of the children, then took the rest to our Children's Village. Unfortunately the stories don't always end so well. On a later rescue, I sent a runner in a couple of days ahead of my soldiers and me to search for the kids who'd been scattered in a raid. We heard there were abandoned children in the area but didn't know exactly where or how many. Based on what the runner told us, I figured we'd find five or ten kids. When we got in, we discovered more than forty. The sight of so many children all alone absolutely floored me. I started checking the kids over for wounds. Everyone there had something wrong, and many had more than one problem. They were wounded, sick, malnourished, and infested with worms.

What could I do? I had room to take a dozen back with me if we packed them in, but they all needed attention, food, medical treatment, and shelter. I picked out fifteen kids who seemed to be in the worst shape and wedged them into the truck one by one until I couldn't fit any more. That meant I had to leave more than twenty behind. I saw flashes of fear in the eyes of the children around the vehicle waiting to get in. Under furrowed brows all those little eyes blinked up at me questioning, *Why are you leaving me? When will you be back? Will you be back?*

When the kids remaining realized I was leaving without them, they started to panic. They started shouting and crying, holding out their arms to me. I couldn't understand the words they were saying, but "No! No! Please don't leave me!" feels the same in every language. Tears streamed from their eyes, making tracks in the dust caking their cheeks. They were hungry and afraid and I was their only hope. Now I was abandoning them. Even though I was taking some of them to safety, my heart broke to leave the rest of them.

Climbing into the Land Cruiser, I looked out at the sea of desperate faces and said, "I'll be back for you. Give me a couple of days, and I'll be back." I was an adult and they wanted to believe me. Maybe they did believe, because the alternative was too scary to think about. But I lied. I had no intention of coming back in two days. I wouldn't be able to return to the area that soon.

A week or so later the LRA hit that area again and killed several people, including some of the children I left behind. I was shaking with rage. "I swear to you, God," I said through my tears, "I will never leave a child behind again as long as I live. Next time I'll get all the weapons and ammo I can and stay behind with them, wait with them for the truck to come back. This will never happen again. Never again!" I had told all those pairs of fearful eyes that I would be back for them. They trusted me—because they had no one else to trust— and I let them down.

I still see those eyes sometimes.

Back in Pennsylvania after that trip, I stayed messed up more than I'd ever been. I kept seeing those little faces; I heard my own lie ringing in my head over and over. I didn't want to talk to people at church about it, didn't want to dis- cuss it when I was speaking on the road, didn't want to talk about it to anybody. I wanted the world to leave me alone. All I wanted was to get on my bike and ride.

I hadn't had a motorcycle in eighteen years—since before I was married. But after a couple of close calls in Africa, I had told my wife, "Before I get killed I want to start riding again." Lynn smiled and said, "You do whatever you want to." Someone who knew my taste in transportation made a desig- nated gift to our ministry specifically to help me buy a motor- cycle, so in 2004 I'd bought the bike of my dreams—a brand-new Harley. Black, lots of chrome. The bike was a blessed escape once in a while, but, of course, I knew it wasn't the ultimate answer.

Eventually I accepted the fact that I had done all I could in the bush that day and didn't have anything to feel guilty about. My men and I had saved fifteen lives. But I reaf- firmed the promise that I would never abandon a child again. I stood up crying in our church one day and made that vow public. "Before God," I declared, "I'm making a commitment right now: I will never leave another child behind."

To make good on that promise, I have to have a split personality. When I'm at home, I think about the orphanage and the children in Nimule. I'm constantly on the phone to Sudan dealing long-distance with its challenges and decisions. When I'm in Africa, I worry about Lynn and Paige and our ministry in Central City. I lie awake in my *tukul* long past midnight thinking about my wife running our local ministry on her own and my daughter growing up without her father so much of the time. Juggling two worlds is hard, especially when both worlds need me at the same time. In some situations one of them gets shortchanged, no matter how hard I try.

Probably the most painful instance of being pulled in two directions at once was when Lynn's son, Wayne, died in 2004. Wayne had moved in with us after we settled in Pennsylvania and stayed until he was fourteen or fifteen. He had gotten pretty rebellious by then and didn't like the rules in our house. Since his father didn't have so many rules, he went to live with him. Wayne was basically a good kid and a hard worker. He got married and had a daughter, Faith, but when his wife went to jail, he couldn't take care of their child by himself. The state was going to take her if Wayne didn't do something, so he called his mother. Lynn and I talked about it and decided, "We'll take her. That's what families do. Let's just go pick her up." We went to Wayne's house in Daytona Beach and got her at Christmas. Wayne signed his parental rights over to us.

Three months later, Wayne died of a heroin overdose. He and his friends had been partying for days. He passed out, and his heart was really racing, so somebody gave him an injection of heroin to slow the heart rate down. I know this can work because I've done the same thing to other people. When they saw that his heart rate had slowed down, they put him in the bed, but nobody went back to check on him. His heart kept slowing down and slowing down until he died.

This all happened right as I was getting ready to go back to Africa. As badly as Lynn needed me, I couldn't postpone my trip because of some crucial things going on over there. I had to be two places at once, and it was impossible. I literally left Wayne's casket at the funeral to go to the airport. A week or two after I got home again Lynn basically had a nervous breakdown. I put her on a plane and sent her to her mom's for a while to rest and recover.

I switch back and forth between being a husband, father, and minister in America and a soldier and commander living by the gun in Africa. Strange as it sounds, after I've been in the U.S. for a while I start longing for Africa; I feel that African part of me straining to come out. Three months at home and I start missing Deng and Guk and Nineteen and Slinky. Start thinking about another rescue.

It's so hard to tell people at home what life is like in Uganda and Sudan. They have no point of reference to understand how desperate the people are, how much they need, and how far even the smallest donation will stretch. I get in the pulpit to preach, and cry out of my own emotion and memories, but also out of frustration and confusion. I can't really explain what it's like to be in Sudan leading a rescue with an AK in my hands and a pistol on each hip, and standing in a pulpit in Central City two days later.

People in the church talk about being "soldiers of Christ." While the phrase can have several different meanings, in my case I take it literally. But I don't believe I'm doing any more than Jesus would do if he were here. If he knew children were being kidnapped and tortured, do you think he would just walk by? The Good Samaritan lay on the road robbed and wounded while a priest and a Levite walked right by. Would Jesus walk to the other side of the road or would he go help that person? Jesus would do the same thing most of us would do.

Some still say, "I don't believe Jesus would go fight." I agree. He probably wouldn't. He probably wouldn't have to. He could turn water into wine. He'd handle it some other way.

I'm no theologian, but I know what I know. The fighting we've done in Uganda and Sudan has produced an oasis of peace and safety in a very dangerous part of the world. If you were to visit there today you could see it for yourself.

A day at the Shekinah Fellowship Children's Center starts right when the sun begins to come up. That's when the ladies of the compound start arriving. Sixteen women do the cooking and washing and take care of the children. They are the hardest-working people I know in Sudan. They work from sunup till sundown at the compound and still take care of their own families.

The first chore of the morning is to boil water for breakfast. The cooks fix tea and porridge, which is oatmeal with a consistency like grits that they drink straight out of the bowl. The ladies add sugar to it. Though the average child in Sudan only eats once a day, this is the first of three daily meals we feed our kids. The workers themselves have tea and bread.

While the ladies are getting breakfast on, the children start to come out of their dormitories to wash up. Everybody in Sudan loves taking care of their teeth. I don't know why, but you never have to tell a child there to go brush his teeth. They're excited about it. After they wash up they have their breakfast, then the older ones leave for school in town.

We pay school fees for the older kids and buy their uniforms, of which they're always proud. Many of them have never belonged to anything; having a uniform is exciting because it shows they're students in a school where they fit in and belong. After school they come back for a late lunch and have playtime. Right before dark, shortly before bedtime, they eat again. The basic diet for lunch and dinner is beans and maize bread, which is a flatbread made from white cornmeal. Sometimes we have rice, and twice a week we have meat and fish. We also serve a vegetable twice a week—usually cabbage but sometimes greens.

Sometimes visitors to the compound want to know why we don't feed the children meat and vegetables every day. The reason is that it's expensive and logistically almost impossible. As I mentioned earlier, besides feeding the children and the workers, we feed anyone in the neighborhood who comes at mealtime, which adds up to about fifteen hundred meals a day. You butcher a cow in the morning, and it's all gone by bedtime. There's no refrigeration, and transportation is expensive, so we have to depend on what we can get locally in large quantities. The beans and maize bread are some of the most nourishing food you can get. Besides, it's actually pretty tasty.

Our youngest children sleep on grass mats on the floor until they stop wetting the bed. As soon as they're old enough, they get a bed. The smallest ones sleep two or three to a bed, while the bigger ones have a bed to themselves. The average Sudanese child sleeps on the bare floor of a *tukul*. Our children all have sheets, towels, blankets, and mosquito nets. There's so much more that we need, but our children are double and triple blessed over anyone else in our area.

The youngest children are toddlers, and the oldest are teenagers. Three of them, James, Francis, and John, were child soldiers, all taught to kill with clubs, machetes, and guns. James, who is eleven years old, killed more than thirty people during his military career. Francis told me that Joseph Kony and his men set up an ambush to kill me on the road, and that Kony was upset when nobody could kill me. That was the time we drove through a group of LRA who looked down and never raised their weapons. Francis said nobody had the power to lift a gun. I never knew about the ambush until he told me.

We have a Sudanese nurse who works at our clinic every day, taking care of the inevitable cuts and bruises as well as sickness, scorpion bites, and whatever else turns up. We also have a woman who teaches the girls when they start to become young ladies, helping them in certain things that the men (our nurse is a man) cannot teach.

That clinic today isn't far from the tree where I hung my mosquito net the first night I spent on the children's center property. I always show it to visitors because it's so hard to imagine Ben and me clearing a path to it and clearing a spot in the grass to stretch out. The cleared spot of ground now stretches hundreds of yards in every direction, even beyond the compound fence. Inside the compound, the roads are smooth and safe—not a boulder in sight—made of packed dirt lined in some places with bricks. Rows of trees grow along the perimeter, and hedges and blooming shrubs spring up around some of the buildings.

Those early *tukuls* have been rebuilt out of fired bricks and tin. Some of the older children live in them now. We have dormitories and are scrounging for funds to build new ones all the time. Each one-story dorm costs about twenty-two thousand dollars. The sturdy, fired-brick buildings are inviting, with stucco on the front painted ochre; doors, window shutters, and trim are a contrasting cheerful blue that resists fading, even in the merciless African sun. Cool, welcoming porches all along the front have concrete floors and metal poles to support the tin roofs overhead. Inside, the furniture is plain but serviceable and the rooms dark and comparatively cool in the daytime heat. Along each wall there are bunk beds stacked two or three high, each with its own mosquito net.

The dining halls are designed a lot like the dorms, including paint colors, and they are furnished with rows of long trestle tables and benches where the children eat their meals. Our simple kitchens use the local style of wood-burning oven. It's low tech, the simplest and most reliable way to prepare our meals. The cooks do a lot of their work outside because it's so hot. Many of the ladies

Sam's daughter Paige, helping out with the Mobile Clinic. Paige now works full-time for the mission and will be starting her own mission work in Africa later this year.

From 1999 to 2002 Sam ran the Mobile Clinic. For many, this was the only medical care they received—regardless of how ill they were.

A typical gathering of villagers seeking medical treatment wait patiently in the shade.

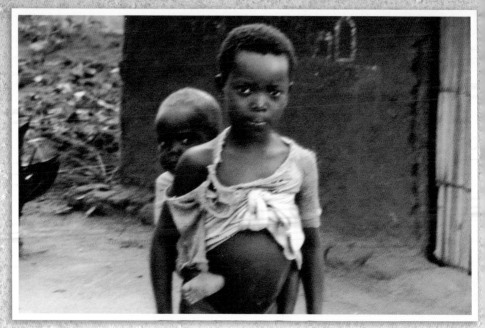

Many of the children we rescue have nowhere else to go, since families are often hesitant to take on another mouth to feed.

Children sharing a bottle of water and a snack

Surviving in the bush often means eating whatever you can find.

Finding clean drinking water in the bush is nearly impossible. This man will drink from and bathe in this pond, just like everyone else.

(top) Sam and his soldiers examine the massive tracks of a python that entered the village one night.

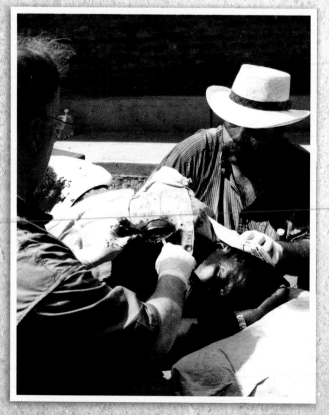

(left) An SPLA soldier is getting sewn up after a bullet shattered his bone.

Kevin Evans

Children who are rescued often weep for days, as they remember all that they have seen . . . and lost.

Kevin Evans

Some of the children from Sam's orphanage, Children's Village

Sam with Lexson Night and Peter Atem surveying the remnants of the war in Southern Sudan.

Sam, at the River Nile, during a day of intense fighting with the LRA.

Kevin Evans

Sam with one of the 1,000-plus children that he has rescued.

Kevin Evans

Sam giving the benediction after a service at the church orphanage. Since Sam started his ministry and crusades in Sudan over 50,000 people have given their hearts to the Lord.

Rhett "Rott" Rotten signs "The African Bike" before his ride on the "Wall of Death."

Sam with Rhett Rotten and his crew to discuss the music for the "Wall of Death" show. After the show Sam was able to minister to the crowd.

"The African Bike" is traveling across the country until June 27, 2009, visiting fairs, churches, concerts, college campuses, and other events. For a $20 donation people can purchase a raffle ticket to win the bike at the big drawing in Johnstown, PA at Thunder in the Valley. To make a donation or get involved check out Sam's Web site: boyerspond.com.

who work for us are widows whose husbands have been killed by the LRA. All together we have a staff of about forty-five, including the cooks, teachers, caretakers, security staff, medical staff, and administrators. We are also building a library and have been working on a church building for a long time. We've met in the church's unfinished shell for months because every time we get going on it, something else comes up that we feel like we need to finish first.

Sam Childers enjoys an average evening, sitting on the porch with the children in Sudan.

Outside the gate it's only fifty yards or so to the river, where there always seems to be a crowd of women washing clothes and bathing their children. Chattering nonstop, their musical voices blend with the sound of water flowing by.

Our soccer team is actually the best in the whole area. They're almost undefeated. Sometimes I wonder if that's because these orphans know they have nothing besides what they're playing for, so they try their very best and leave nothing on the field. There's a full-size soccer field and a playground—the first playground in Southern Sudan—with sturdy, first-class equipment anchored in concrete. Swings, slides, seesaws, and a merry-go-round swarm with clusters of the youngest children during the day, while the older ones are away at school. They return in the afternoon to do their lessons, practice soccer in their flashy green and white uniforms, or enjoy a little free time of their own.

In 2002 we started securing and guarding the compound.

There are always ten guards on duty, which is an improvement because we used to need twenty. We were able to cut back because fighting in our area isn't as bad as it used to be; the government now keeps a platoon of soldiers outside our fence within a hundred yards of our gate. We used to have machine guns posted at the fence, but those are now unnecessary. Four guards patrol and man the gate during the day, and six walk the perimeter at night; all ten live with us on the compound.

When there's no LRA activity, the nights are peaceful and relatively cool. The only electricity we have is what we generate ourselves; in order to save money we run our generator no more than three hours or so per day. From dusk on we have electricity for a while, but we try to rely on fires and flashlights until the adults go to bed. I sit around with the soldiers for a while and listen for any signs of enemy activity. The African night is so vast it still impresses me. When I'm sitting around the fire with the troops, it's easy to look up at the sky and remember spending my first night in this place. Then I look around and see all the dormitories, roads, warehouses, and everything else we've built in the past ten years and can hardly get my head around what a miracle it all is.

The African night sleeps. The singing and laughing and giggling in the dormitories have wound down. Three hundred young souls—bellies filled, teeth brushed—snuggle down under warm blankets on soft, clean sheets for a safe night's rest. For some, old terrors come back as nightmares, shocking them awake with a gasp or a scream. They are too young to have gone through what they have, too young to have lived such dark days with horrific memories burned into their minds. A comforting hand reaches out. A bunkmate calls out quietly, "It's only a dream. *Tom-Tom* can never get you here. The soldiers are with us. God is with us. You are safe."

The big, open, cooking fireplaces glow in the darkness, coals banked, at rest after a busy day. The skilled hands of the cooks that command them rest nearby, fifteen hundred meals behind them today and another fifteen hundred ahead of them after the next sunrise. Widows of war—victims themselves—these women find purpose and fulfillment in their task.

And so here sleeps my life's work. A little oasis of safety and assurance in a sea of war and danger. A light for Christ in a murky and troubled land. A calm and fearless outpost of hope in the middle of another man's war.

EIGHT
the call

In under three years, Clyde had taken me from a wasted drug abuser to a partner in a successful business. He taught me how to do the work better and more efficiently, how to manage a job, how to do an estimate—everything I needed to run the show on my own. I had come a long way and was making more money than ever, but my life still wasn't right. I was still spending lots of time in bars, still fighting, still selling drugs and doing half an ounce or an ounce of cocaine every day myself. I knew I had to get out of Florida for the same reason I'd left Minnesota years before: either I was going to kill myself with drugs or somebody was going to kill me in a fight.

When Clyde died in 1985 I actually inherited his business; but instead of staying to run it, I got somebody else to come in and manage it for Clyde's widow. That ended up being a big mistake. The new manager stole from her and was sued. Instead of bringing Clyde's old gear to Pennsylvania, I sold it—along with what I already had of my own—and went to Central City with brand-new tools and equipment. Lynn and I sold our furniture and everything else we had and moved to Central City that summer.

When I started setting up my business and looking for work, my headquarters was a little eight-by-eight shed beside my parents' garage. I kept a hot tar kettle for roofing and my other tools there. When winter came, I realized there wasn't going to be any work during the cold weather in Pennsylvania, so I went back to Florida to do roofing and outside construction for the season. When I returned north in the spring of 1986, I brought a pound and a half of marijuana with me. I sold a lot of it in those days. Sometimes I brought it home myself, and sometimes my friend Delane boxed it up—packed with coffee to hide the smell—and sent it to me via UPS. By repackaging pounds of it into dime bags—ten dollars' worth that would make eight or ten joints—I was making a pile of money.

Around that time I had a change of heart about doing hard drugs. Clyde had showed me I could be better tomorrow than I was yesterday, and I decided that part of being better was to get off hard drugs. I still smoked a lot of weed and still loved to fight, but I pretty much got off of cocaine and other really dangerous narcotics.

I had come to a turning point in my life; I wanted something more.

I didn't go through any sort of program or see a doctor or counselor, though I think that way works for a lot of people and it's what they need to do. There are certain drugs, like heroin, that can cause extreme withdrawal symptoms, but for me, getting off cocaine and the other stuff I was doing was a matter of mental strength. It was like an overeater wanting a cream-filled donut. He doesn't want one or two; he wants six, and knows he can't eat one or else he'll end up with six. I had to say in my mind that I was not going to do any hard drugs at all anymore. That's how I stopped. I didn't know about God's sovereignty then or how the Bible talks about us controlling our bodies. Ultimately God is in control, but he puts each of us in charge of what we think and what our bodies do. At the time, I believed that I was in complete control of my body and that I could choose to say no to drugs. For me, it was a matter of willpower.

Before long, Childers Roofing and Painting was going great guns. I took on concrete work and started putting up pole buildings as well; later I went into excavating. I hired more workers and bought more equipment. Eventually I expanded to where I owned two bulldozers, two dump trucks, a backhoe, a crane, and a lot of other gear. I hired one man just to keep it all running and another just to help me drive. Clyde's business lessons were putting food on our table, and that gave me a burst of confidence in my own abilities.

I started running a pawnshop out of my company office. The pawnshop was so successful, I branched out into real estate by buying a couple of old company houses in coal mining towns. I soon found that I could snap up houses for as little as three thousand dollars. Granted, these houses needed a lot of work, but I had my own construction crew, so I was able to fix them up and sell them at a profit. My dad went in with me on some of these.

Then I started buying all the old houses I could, fixing them up, and financing them back to the sellers for a thousand dollars down. They had a like-new house for a monthly payment lower than rent, and I had a steady investment income that didn't require me to lift a finger. I owned about twenty of these when I stopped doing it after a few years; it was too much hassle. I had been doing a lot of the work myself, but the company was getting so big I was sending workers down to do what I should have been doing. I started fading out of the real estate business, but I made some good money while I was at it.

This isn't to say everything about my life was rosy. I was still drinking and smoking pot, same as I'd been doing forever, and I still fought a lot—not because I got into rough situations or because I was defending an underdog, but because I liked fighting. Lynn had become a Christian in the fall of 1987 and, as I've already said, I was jealous of God for the time he spent with her when she and I could have been fishing or shopping for antiques. We argued about it sometimes. I never hurt her physically, but I had a nasty temper and let her know exactly how I felt.

About that time, God decided what he wanted to change next about me and how to get my attention in order to do it. Lynn wanted us to have a baby but we couldn't seem to get pregnant. We both thought it would be wonderful if Wayne could have a little brother or sister. That wasn't the way it turned out though. It looked like maybe there was something wrong, and we wouldn't be able to conceive a child the old-fashioned way, so we decided to try in vitro fertilization. To have the best chance of success I had to quit all drugs, quit drinking, and even quit smoking cigarettes. I wanted a baby, too, and figured it was worth it if that would do the trick.

As time passed without a pregnancy, Lynn got sadder and more frustrated. Some of her God stuff had started to

126

affect me a little, and I started praying at night that he would bring us a child. One night, lying upstairs in my bedroom, I made a deal. I said, "Lord, if you allow my wife to get pregnant and you allow us to have a child, I will never do drugs or drink again." Not too long after that came the fantastic day when the doctor said my wife was pregnant. My prayer was answered, and I kept my end of the bargain. Since that day I haven't had so much as a beer. On May 15, 1989, our daughter, Paige, was born.

—

Three years later, in the summer of 1992, I gave my heart to the Lord during a revival at the Assembly of God church on the same night the pastor prophesied I would go with him to Africa. While I thought the whole Africa thing was crazy then, I did feel in my heart that the time had come for me to be a pastor. He was calling me in the same little town where I had first felt the tug of the ministry during my great-grandmother's funeral so many years ago.

Since that long-ago day, I had turned away from that calling more times than I could count. Yet I had felt it fleetingly, even during those wild and lost years. It happened once when I was running from some Indians on a Minnesota reservation. I ran off the highway and into the woods to try and lose my pursuers. I had my duffel bag with me, and I groped frantically inside the bag for the sawed-off 12-gauge I knew was there—somewhere. Pounding through the underbrush and trying to watch where I was going, I was fishing around in my bag for my gun, yanking out clothes and tossing them aside, when my hand hit an old Bible my mom had given me.

"God," I said, "you're going to have to do something now!" I figured with the Bible, God, and the 12-gauge I was about as safe as I could get, though I have to admit I was counting on the shotgun most.

When I finally did become a Christian, I couldn't get enough of it. I started studying the Bible really seriously and taking Bible school courses at home. I wanted to know everything.

If God is my master, I wondered, *what are my instructions?*

It was about a year before I got an answer to that question. I was in the Rocky Mountains of Colorado on an elk hunt. It was a crisp, clear, beautiful day with snow on the ground and a dusting on the tall fir and spruce trees all around me, just below the timberline. I was carrying one of my favorite guns in the world, a Weatherby .340 Magnum, which I consider to be the best elk rifle on the planet. I sat down on a log to smoke a cigarette and, out of nowhere, felt the presence of God beside me.

God said, *You know, it's time for you to start preaching.*

I wasn't so sure. I still wasn't completely living the life I thought a preacher should live; besides, I still smoked. I don't think there's anything in the Bible against smoking, but I didn't know of any Assembly of God preachers who smoked. At least any who admitted to it. I said, "Yeah, right. I'm sitting here smoking a cigarette and you're telling me I'm to start preaching."

God said, *I will take care of that problem.* He told me the exact day I would quit smoking and he handled it from then on. He took care of the hardest part of my cigarette addiction and left me to do the rest. I had been smoking three packs a day, including probably half a pack at night. I would wake up, smoke a cigarette, and go back to sleep. God took away my craving for cigarettes at night. When that happened I knew it was up to me to keep away from them during the day. I struggled at first, but once I stopped I never put another cigarette to my lips.

Do I believe cigarettes are a sin? They're no more of a sin than overeating or anything else we overindulge in. It becomes a sin when it keeps us from more important things. I believe cigarettes, TV, and a long list of other diversions can turn into sins if they keep us from a relationship with God, especially when he has called us to serve him.

Sitting there on the log in the middle of the Rockies, I knew that my life was about to drastically change. I was ready to begin my ministry as a preacher, but I wanted to ask for one favor first.

"God," I said, "I have no problem obeying you and starting to preach. I'll tell you, though, I've been coming out here to hunt in Colorado for years and I love it. If I start preaching, I'm not going to be able to get back here again for a long time—maybe never. So let me shoot a big elk today."

Just as I said that, a monster elk came into view about five hundred yards away. He walked down a ridge, perfectly outlined against the cold, brilliant, dark blue sky. I dropped him with one shot. His mounted head and huge rack are on the wall of my living room today.

As the idea of starting a ministry sank in, I felt the need to prepare a place to do the work. In 1995 I bought forty acres across the highway from my construction company office and my house—forty acres of rolling hills covered with sandy soil and shaded by a thick canopy of tall trees. The forest kept it cool and breezy in summer, and when the snow came it looked like a Christmas card. I wanted a campground where people could meet to study, pray, and enjoy each other's fellowship. The next year I put in a septic system, and we started having regular camp meetings on that land.

I talked to my pastor, Dean Krause, a wise counselor and mentor who supported my desire to be in ministry from the first time we discussed it, although I was still a little rough around the edges. One day I was in church at the altar praying and weeping. He came over and knelt down beside me to pray with me; he laid his hand on my back and felt my shoulder harness holding the pistol I always carried. Then he moved his hand down and felt another pistol in the small of my back. He glanced over at me, muffled a chuckle, and said, "Here I am praying with some guy at the altar, crying and praying and shouting out to God—and he's got a gun on each side of him!" He always remembered that.

I believe guns can teach principles of Christianity in a unique way, especially to people who know more about guns than they do about the Bible.

Think about the Holy Trinity. The Father is Father God. The Holy Spirit is like a bodyguard who tells us in our minds when we're about to do wrong. Jesus is the Son of God; we have to go through him to get to the Father. The parts of the Trinity work together like you or me firing a pistol. There's the pistol, the bullet, and the hand. With the pistol empty, it won't work even if there's a hand to fire it. A hand just holding the bullet in its palm is useless without the pistol. A loaded pistol lying on the counter won't fire by itself. It takes all three: the gun, the bullet, and the hand. I've used that as a demonstration many times over the years. It might seem a little crazy, but a gun takes all three components in order to become effective, and that's what I believe about the Trinity.

God gave me the wisdom to recognize the need to use a gun to do his work in Africa, the knowledge of how to use one, and the faith to take one into dangerous situations. He allowed me to use it to protect myself and continue my work there. I do not believe that Jesus Christ ever condoned violence or told us to go out and murder, but he does want us to protect our families. To me that family includes the children of Africa. Jesus said that any man who does not take care of his family is worse than an infidel.

To someone who thinks a preacher shouldn't be armed to go into the African bush and rescue a child, let me ask you this: What if it was your child? What if it was your young boy or girl who was kidnapped and you knew where the child was and knew he or she was in danger? Say someone like me came along and said, "Ma'am, I can go get your child. I will bring your child home to you tomorrow." Would you say, "No, don't do that. I don't condone violence"? Or would you weep and beg, "Yes, please, bring my child home!"? My guess is that you'd say, "Bring him home." So as I kept preparing for the ministry, I saw no reason to give up guns and fighting. The more I learned, the more I saw the need for them.

I applied for a license to preach with the Independent Assemblies of Pennsylvania in 1998 and preached under their oversight for two years. After that, I was talking to Pastor Krause one day and he said, "Sam, let us license you." I thought that was a good idea, and from then until now I've been licensed through the Abundant Life Fellowship out of Phillipsburg, Pennsylvania. Dean still mentors me, and to this day I'm accountable as a pastor to him and his fellowship. We still talk, and he still gives me his opinion. We don't always see eye to eye (I don't think he ever started carrying a pistol in the pulpit), but he's always there for me.

During these years you could say my life took a completely different direction. Then again, you could also say it was going in every direction at once. At the end of 1998, as I've already mentioned, I made my first trip to the Sudan. For the next three years I went back and forth to Africa, developed my campground in Central City, started building a church on the property, and ran my construction business. In 2000 I started driving the mobile clinic in Sudan and also began construction of the orphanage in Nimule.

On August 19, 2001, we had the first service in our church at the campground in Central City, which we named Shekinah Fellowship Church. The building was a long way from finished, but we couldn't have been prouder of it if it had been a stone cathedral. All we had at first was the basement with a poured concrete floor, painted concrete block walls, and a temporary roof. The basement was on a hillside so that one end had doors and windows and sunlight filtering through the trees, while the other end was underground. We planned to put up a permanent roof as soon as we could, which would eventually be the floor of the sanctuary upstairs.

Later that year in October, Lynn and Paige went with me to Africa and were there when the first handful of children came to live at the orphanage. The first day we were there, I was preaching under a tree when the LRA bombed the area—not once, but six times. I kept right on preaching, and the locals never forgot that. It showed them that I was serious about my work, and that I had no fear of the LRA.

Up to this point, my personal savings and profits from my construction company had paid for all my work in Africa plus the land and building for Shekinah Fellowship. Lynn and I started a newsletter, but no one was really out there trying to raise money. I couldn't keep preaching and supporting my African mission without money, but I couldn't make money if I was spending all my time preaching and going to Africa. To answer the call on my life, I had to move ahead on faith alone. Two of my employees agreed to buy the construction company from me. I set that process in motion, but at the last minute they changed their minds. There was no turning back for me then, so I had an auction and sold my vehicles, tools, and equipment. Financially it was a disaster. I had brand-new merchandise going for a quarter of what I'd paid for it. Air compressors still in crates went for $120. I went behind the building where no one could see me and cried so hard. The hope had been to get a big financial boost for my ministry, but it didn't happen, and now I was out of business. I'd just sold the goose whose golden eggs had kept everything going.

After some lean and difficult years, God blessed our ministry. He had to be sure I was in all the way, in for keeps.

I was able to hang in there because I had a call. That's the most important part of becoming a pastor—you have to be sure without a shred of doubt that God has called you to preach. When God has you in his grip, you can't help serving him. It becomes the most important thing in your life. In my case answering the call meant more than my business, more than my financial security, even more than my family.

When there's a call on our lives, it stays there waiting patiently, no matter how long it takes for us to pick up on it. I could have spent my whole life pastoring a church or running a ministry, but I missed my first call. And the second. And the third, fourth, and fifth. Because I missed all those opportunities, when I finally did surrender to God, I felt a real passion that he had to use what was left. Even though there were a lot of scars and a lot of bad things in my past, I believe God looked at me and said, "There's still something there in Sam Childers for me to work with."

So he began to clean that up and mold it. Once he starts working with something, he's not going to leave it the same. I absolutely believe that a normal preacher with a college education could never do what I do. Not because he doesn't have the desire, but because he's not equipped with the experience God has given me. Had I died during those years, I would surely have gone to hell. God's mercy won't keep you out of hell when you're intentionally sinning as I was. But once I surrendered to him, a new plan came into play, and a new ministry was born.

Romans 11:29 says, "The gifts and the calling of God are irrevocable." Maybe you know inside that you have a call on your life, but you feel as though you've lost it or deserted it or missed your chance. Believe me when I tell you that the call is still there. He will never take away the gifts and the call he gave me, and the same is true for you.

Because I left all God's earlier assignments behind, I have this new assignment he gave me. And it's not an assignment for the healthy; it's only for the sick. In Matthew 9:13, Jesus said, "Go and learn what this means: 'I desire mercy and not sacrifice.' For I did not come to call the righteous, but sinners, to repentance." God doesn't call people who think they're righteous; he calls people who know they're sinners. I was as bad as they come, which makes it clear why God called me: he called me to go out and speak to others who are sinners.

Romans 8:27–28 is a great scripture that says, "Now He [God] who searches the hearts knows what the mind of the Spirit is, because He makes intercession for the saints according to the will of God. And we know that all things work together for good to those who love God, to those who are the called according to His purpose." I absolutely believe that every time I made a mistake, God was saying, "Boy, this guy messed up again! But I'm still going to use him!"

Once he called me, I was his forever. Now I'm serving him wherever he can use me. For the time being, that means having one foot in the Stony Creek of eastern Pennsylvania and the other foot in the Nile.

NINE

in the palm of his hand

When I started building the Children's Village in Southern Sudan, there was no master plan on paper, no blueprints for buildings. I had nothing figured out ahead of time, the way it would normally be done. God gave me the whole idea in a vision one night. I made a map of it according to his instructions, and that's all I ever used to work from. I still have the map. The campground in Pennsylvania had been the same way—a one-night vision. I didn't sit down and say, "The cabins go here, the playground goes here, and the church goes here." God told me what he wanted, and that's what I did.

After those early *tukuls* in 2000 and 2001, a few workers and I started building little staff houses for workers, then bigger houses, and the first dormitories for the children after that. The dormitories were simple, sturdy, rectangular buildings. The window openings had shutters but no glass, which is common in the African countryside. Glass is expensive, hard to get, dangerous when it's broken, and too easily shattered with children scrambling all over the place. Since it never gets cold, and the eaves keep out the rain, shutters alone provide plenty of protection. We needed a bathhouse and a kitchen, so we built those as well. We cleared ground as fast as we could with the hand tools available. Foot by foot, yard by yard, we'd get another tangle of underbrush cut down and uprooted until we had an acre of it cleaned off. Then we started on the next acre.

Once I started getting settled, I felt it was very important to build a good relationship with the Sudanese People's Liberation Army as soon as I could. I had heard some criticism of the SPLA and knew that other missionaries weren't helping them. They were technically a rebel force at the time, formed in opposition to the regular Sudanese army, but I never had any problem with the SPLA. In fact, I was impressed with how they were trying to protect the adults and children in the area. It was only later that we learned the full extent of the regular Sudanese army's terrible mistreatment of their own people in Darfur and elsewhere as they tried to enforce the official Islamic legal code.

I had SPLA soldiers with me from the first time I went to Africa. Once they realized I was as committed to helping the people of Sudan as they were, they accepted me as their friend and fellow soldier. When I saw that they didn't have the equipment and supplies they needed in the field, I started bringing them gifts like binoculars, tents, and sleeping bags.

I started hiring the SPLA for security work, and because we worked so close together, I became an SPLA soldier myself. They saw that my heart was to make a difference in the lives of their people, so they started calling me a commander. I carried truckloads of food, salt, sugar, blankets, and other supplies to the front for soldiers, as well as preaching to them and encouraging them in battle.

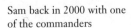
Sam back in 2000 with one of the commanders

Naturally the Lord's Resistance Army didn't like having a Christian *mzunga* in the neighborhood spoiling their fun. The Sudanese government had left them alone, thinking that if the LRA harassed the southerners who wouldn't convert to Islam, government soldiers wouldn't have to spend their time doing it.

The LRA continued trying to attack our compound but never succeeded. They also tried more than once to kill me. One of the times, I was walking with a couple of my men from the compound to the river. The area there had been cleared so the enemy couldn't hide in the undergrowth. We hadn't seen any activity or heard of any LRA nearby in the past few days.

Without warning I heard zzzzzzzZZZZTT whizzing past my ear, maybe two inches from my head. A rifle crack followed a millisecond later. The old saying that "there's no need to duck because you never hear the one that gets you" is absolutely true; bullets travel three times the speed of sound. But I ducked anyway, fell to one knee, and yanked my .357 from its holster. As I transitioned from standing to kneeling, I fired off two rounds. The two solders with me shouldered their AK-47s and sprayed the bush with lead. Since we never heard anyone run and never found a body, we figured he must have gotten away that time.

As word of our ministry got around, we became more popular, the number of children living at the orphanage grew, and the LRA tried even harder to kill me. When they saw they could never successfully attack the orphanage, they attacked a nearby village and started asking them about me—where I was and how many soldiers I had—to set up another attempt on my life. At the time I was planning what I called a crusade, a small-scale version of the events Billy Graham had held for so many years with several nights of music and preaching. Somebody claiming to represent the LRA called the radio station in Gulu and told them they would kill me if I went through with my plans.

People said I should cancel. "Kony hates you," they said. "Kony's out to take care of you for good, and he'll do it!"

I didn't care.

First of all, I figured that after everything God had brought me through to get to this point, he'd never give me up to one loony rebel commander. Second, I had never run from a fight in my life, and I wasn't going to start now. I was here to fight another man's war, fighting for children and innocent victims who couldn't fight for themselves, and staying the course until the war was over. I told them, "If we don't have this crusade, people will think the god Joseph Kony serves is greater than our God." There was no way we could allow that. Our presentation went ahead exactly as planned, and we didn't have any trouble.

The local witch doctors were less dangerous but just as opposed to our faith. Witch doctors are powerful and influential figures in the villages, jealous of anything that might diminish their standing in the eyes of their people. They call on spirits to bring good luck, heal the sick, ensure victory in battle, and ease the pain of childbirth (among other things) using a combination of chants, powders, potions, dances, icons, and trinkets. To them, pills and shots are dangerous and unproven—Christianity, even more so.

Not long after the orphanage opened, I was in a village near Yei when the people there told me their witch doctor wanted to kill me. He'd had enough of *mzunga* spirits and medicine, and was ready to get rid of the competition. The villagers had no doubt he could cast a spell and finish me off. As I stood talking with a family in the doorway of their *tukul*, who should come around the corner but Mr. Witch Doctor himself.

He stopped twenty feet or so away and we stood there looking at each other. Everybody within sight of us quit what they were doing to turn and watch. The witch doctor didn't wear any clothes but was covered with necklaces and wrist and ankle ornaments made out of feathers and bones. His wrinkled skin and white hair gave him an air of age and wisdom, but his eyes were wide like a madman. Nobody moved for a beat or two, then the witch doctor jumped straight up in the air and back down again—exactly like a cartoon character—and started dancing and jumping toward me, waving his hands and shouting; he was giving me the full treatment. He threw a bag of bones at my feet, chanting and dancing around me. I shoved him in the chest, really just to push him away, but he reacted as though a mighty force had pushed him. He went flying backward, started yelling again, scrambled to his feet, and ran away as fast as he could. The people in the village who had been hiding in their huts and peeking out their doors at the action poured outside, raising their hands and shouting with joy and excitement.

I couldn't explain what happened then, and I can't explain it now, other than to say I believe God showed the power of his presence to that witch doctor and his followers.

That was only a warm-up to another experience I had later that same year. I'm not asking you to believe or not believe anything; I'm just telling you what happened to me.

One night I went into my *tukul* and locked it from the inside. While I was sleeping, I felt something evil entering my room. That's the only way I can describe it. It wasn't a dream; it wasn't my imagination; it was a real presence, and it radiated evil in dark, sinister rays. I woke up with a start, and as I groped around in the dark for my flashlight and pistol, God said to me, *No, you begin to pray.*

I started to argue. I wanted to see what was waiting at the foot of the bed to attack me, and I wanted to blow it to smithereens. But God was serious. It was kind of like when my parents used to holler at me; there was one holler that could be ignored without great consequence. But there was another tone of voice that you recognized immediately, stopping you in your tracks. That's what happened that night.

I said, "No, Lord, I want to see what just came in the room."

The Lord answered, *No, start praying now.*

I began to pray, pray, pray in the pitch dark, and after about three hours I prayed myself to sleep. When I woke up the next morning, I sat on the bed and rubbed my head.

Wow, man, I thought to myself. *Was that a dream? What happened?* I looked down at the concrete floor, and what I saw sent goose bumps shooting up my arms and all the way down my back: there was an unbroken, perfectly mounded circle of gray ash running the whole way around the bed. The line was about half an inch high and an inch wide. I started to cry.

"Lord, what happened?" I asked. My voice was so tight it came out in a ragged croak.

God said, *Satan came to kill you last night, but he could not cross the blood line. He went around and around the bed, trying to break through, but he couldn't break through my power.*

I believe the ashes marked an invisible blood line around me created by prayer, and I believe Satan just kept going around and around and around my bed in a circle trying to get across it. I believe he could have broken through if I had stopped praying. Satan was waiting for it to be broken, and he was causing so much steam and power that it left a trail of burnt ash. The door was still bolted from the inside. Just thinking about it makes those goose bumps come back.

Most of my encounters in Africa have been less dramatic. One time early in the ministry, my soldiers Ben and Thomas and I were in Kampala shopping for supplies when a Muslim came into the store and started getting smart with me, criticizing me, criticizing my faith. This is an area where there are a lot of Muslims, so I figured this little guy could cause us some trouble. Sure enough, hearing the commotion, a knot of Muslims gathered around us in the store. In my typical shy and retiring fashion, I picked up an axe handle and put it under the mouthy Muslim's chin; then I threw the handle on the table with a loud clatter. The Muslim and his buddies scattered, and I said a silent prayer. "Thank you, Lord, that the situation was handled without a fight."

But when we left the store and went outside, the street was full of Muslims waiting for me. One of them came up to me and got in my face, running his mouth off about how my God was dead. I started to get hot, but Ben said, "Come on, Pastor, let's go get in the car." I gave the Muslim a look and turned around.

As we started to drive away, another guy stuck his face in the window and shouted, "Your God is dead!" I slammed on the brakes, threw open the door, and jumped out of the car. That startled him. Considering the Muslim mob around us, he wasn't expecting me to do anything.

I headed straight for that little guy and said, "The Lord I serve is the living Lord Jesus. And to show you he's alive, I'm going to send you to meet him right now!" But as I started to grab him, Ben grabbed me.

Ben is a big man and a good fighter. He got a tight grip on my shoulder and said, "Come on, Pastor, get in the car now!" I got back in the car. When I looked out, the street mob, maybe a hundred in all, had clubs and rocks and were getting ready to attack. But we drove off without a single rock being thrown.

As we drove out of town Ben said, "Pastor, I was willing to fight with you or die with you. Today I believe we would have died." Fortunately Ben was there to bring me back to my senses.

That time I avoided a fight. Other times, I didn't.

Before I had my house in Kampala, I was staying in a hotel there. Walking to my room one night, I noticed these two men following me. I stopped at the door before mine and acted like I was getting out my key. The two approached to rob me. As they rushed forward, I grabbed one of them by the back of the neck and slammed his head against the wall as hard as I could. His head hit with a dull thud, and blood spattered everywhere. The other guy turned to run, so I knocked his feet out from under him and, as he fell, I kicked him under the chin as hard as I could with my motorcycle boot. In seconds I had gone from a potential robbery victim to the winner of a two-on-one contest, with both of my opponents bleeding and unconscious on the floor. I got to my room as fast as I could, locked the door, and tried to go to sleep. I didn't sleep much because I kept thinking I heard the guys waking up and heading for my door. Finally I drifted off, and when I woke up the hall was empty. I never saw those two again.

Sometimes the littlest enemies are the most dangerous. One night when Lynn and Paige were with me in Africa, I was lying in bed in the dark and felt something pinching my arm. I reached over with my other hand and felt a spider the size of my hand. I grabbed it and threw it across the room.

145

The next morning there was a hole in my arm with some watery stuff oozing out of it. A few days later there was fever in the wound, and it had turned red and swollen. I knew I was in trouble and had to see what I could do about it, but didn't want the girls to worry. I also didn't want to be so sick I couldn't take care of them.

I felt a knot growing under my skin. At first I thought it was the infection, maybe a knot of pus or something like that. But the more I looked and poked around the open hole in my arm, the more I thought it was something else. At first I actually couldn't bear to tell myself the truth, but the truth was it was a sac of spider eggs living in my arm. Since I could only reach the spot with one hand, I had to get Lynn to help me pull the sac out. I thought, *Let's please be careful and get this thing out of my arm without breaking it.* That was the only thing I could think of that would be worse. We got it out, and as soon as we did, all this blood and water and pus came streaming out. The redness went away almost immediately, and soon my arm was as good as new.

There are a lot of aspects to life in Africa that you have to be willing to look at in a whole new way. Spider bites there set a whole new standard. So does the food. One of the truths you learn in the mission field is, "Where he leads me I will follow, and what he feeds me I will swallow." The African diet is usually maize or maize bread, rice, and beans, with an occasional goat thrown in. It's simple, nourishing, and even tasty, as long as it's fresh, which isn't for very long. Because there's no electricity in much of Africa, there's not much refrigeration; food spoils very quickly in the extreme desert climate. The locals seem to be used to it, but to Westerners who are used to having things sanitary and fresh, eating out in the bush can be a real challenge.

Once, we were traveling through the village of Tali and didn't have a lot of food with us. I was really sick with a fever, I was hungry, and I knew I needed to eat something. I was eating some dried fish I'd gotten there and thought I saw something moving in the fish. I looked a little closer and realized it was maggots. I'd already eaten most of the fish and had surely swallowed handfuls of maggots without realizing it. I wondered how I could stand to be any sicker than I already was. But I never got any sicker.

Another time Deng and I were in the village of Moboko, and we hadn't eaten all day. We bought some food, and I snarfed mine down in no time. As Deng was eating, he looked down and saw maggots all over his meal. I had already eaten all mine, and no doubt had a hearty dose of maggots in the process. I hadn't been sick when I started eating, but the thought of those maggots inside me sure made me feel sick.

I've also eaten bush cat, which looks like a big house cat with a bushy tail. I've eaten dog and monkey, but I couldn't stomach field rats. I've never been so hungry that I would eat one. They gross me out. I've eaten kob, which looks and tastes like deer, really delicious. And I've had termites, which you eat live after pulling the wings off; they are kind of sweet and crunchy. My favorite dish is fish head soup, which is a lot better than it sounds; it's a whole fish cooked with a sauce and then poured over rice.

Through all these experiences—circumstances I'd usually tend to avoid as dangerous, crazy, or both—God has kept me in the palm of his hand. I know he's there because he speaks to me in different ways. He can reach us through our emotions. It can be just having good feelings. Still there have been times when I literally heard the voice of God or the voice of Christ speak, and it is as though he's sitting next to me.

He also speaks to me in a very special way through the children. Once, I returned to the orphanage at night and found a group of children sleeping on the ground outside the gate. Soldiers had kept the gate closed.

I said, "What's going on here?"

One of the soldiers explained, "We didn't want to do anything until we heard from you."

I said, "Open these doors and let the children in!" The soldiers moved quickly, and I turned back to the children. "Come on in!" I said, sweeping them through the gate with my arms.

We had a church service a day or two later, and a little girl about eleven stood up and said, "They wouldn't let me in, but I knew if I waited the gatekeeper would come and he would invite me in."

As she spoke I started to cry. Then a boy about six stood up and said he'd had nowhere to live, so he lived under a tree in the market, living on food that shoppers dropped or left behind. Sometimes people would give him something, and sometimes he would steal. The orphanage was his refuge, his new beginning.

One of God's most surprising messages to me was to spare the life of a murderer whom I was seconds away from killing. The Ugandan government had set up a place in Gulu for LRA commanders who were willing to give themselves up and accept an amnesty agreement. Guards protected them from revenge killings by other LRA honchos until they could settle somewhere else.

An important officer named Sam Kolo had turned himself in. A lot of my children knew him, and said he had hurt them and plenty of other people. The SPLA troops who worked with me—along with everybody else, it seemed—thought Kolo was too mean and had done too much wrong to deserve amnesty.

"This man needs to be killed," they insisted. "Everybody knows this."

If he's that terrible, I thought, *I'll just even things up by taking care of him myself.*

I told my soldiers that we would go to this place in Gulu and say we had come to interview Sam Kolo. We'd say that while we were talking to him, he flipped out and came at us with a knife, so we had to kill him in self-defense. I went there fully intending to leave with this killer's blood on my hands.

The guards knew us and let us go in to interview Kolo without any guards present.

He and I started to talk. There was a frightening coldness about him. I could sense no emotion whatsoever. After a few minutes I asked him, "Don't you have any remorse for what you have done?"

He looked at me and said, "No."

That was all I needed. I had a big knife on me, and at that point I actually reached down and put my hand on the knife. I was going to cut his throat right there.

Then he paused, looked at me for a second, and said, "But you don't understand. I was captured as a child." He started telling me about being captured by the LRA years before and what they'd done to him. He was brainwashed as a boy. He never knew any better. We can say a child knows better, but when you capture a child at eleven years old and start brainwashing him and giving him drugs and making him kill, that child will have no idea of what's right and wrong. A world of killing on command is the only world he knows. That's what happened to Sam Kolo.

I took my hand off my knife. After we sat in silence for a minute I asked, "Do you feel like you need something more in your life?"

"Yes," he answered.

"Have you ever heard about Jesus Christ?"

"I've heard of him a little."

As I started filling in the gaps, Kolo hung on every word. I had come to kill him that day and send him to hell. Instead, I led him to eternal life in heaven. My soldiers stared open-mouthed at the two of us.

Finally Kolo and I parted company, and the soldiers and I headed out to the car. "But Pastor," one of my men said, "I thought we came to kill this man. We're leaving, and we did not do the job!" I didn't know how to explain it. In a weird way I was disappointed because I'd thought so hard about what to do and how to do it. I was so focused on ending this murderer's life, and then I didn't do it. By the time I got back to my house in Gulu I felt God telling me that I *did* kill him. Actually God killed the old Sam Kolo through me. His old life of death and evil was gone, replaced with a new, clean, spotless life in Christ.

If we looked hard at every one of us for all the wrong

we've done—the things we have in our closets, the things we hide, the things we're going to have to answer for one day—there's a lot of us that should be killed. And we were killed when we gave our hearts to Christ. All of the old is gone.

Why is it so easy for God to forgive us of all the dirt that we've done to him and other people, yet it's so hard for us to forgive each other? Even if you're a person who was influenced to murder, he will open his arms to welcome you as quickly as he does anyone else. All sinners are equally damned and everyone, no matter what they've done, can be equally forgiven and blessed.

Africa seems to have more than its share of dirt flying in every direction. That's part of the reason why they're dealing with so many troubles, and why it's so hard to do anything about them.

TEN

war of the words

Follow the trail of any African crisis—lawlessness, poverty, genocide, lack of development, whatever—and you'll probably end up at the same place: politics. With few exceptions, African politics are a messy combination of old tribal conflicts, leftover colonial squabbles, self-perpetuating military dictatorships, and the modern scramble for world oil. Weak governments and corrupt or inept leaders have caused generations of suffering all across the continent, including the bloody guerrilla wars that have victimized children in Uganda and Southern Sudan.

The good news is that both of these countries have been led by gifted, compassionate men—presidents who got to the top by military force but are men of peace who have done great things for their countries. I've had the honor of knowing President Yoweri Museveni of Uganda and the late John Garang, former president of Southern Sudan. I also have a lot of respect for Garang's successor, Salva Kiir Mayadrit. Our orphanage and our ministry would not have the success they've had without the help of these men.

My introduction to African heads of state started with a phone call from the U.S. To help raise money for my work I'd set up a business providing guide services and security for groups traveling in Uganda and Sudan. I had the contacts, I had the soldiers, and I had the guns, so I figured I might as well let other people take advantage of them and bring in a little cash for the children. I got a call from *The 700 Club* on the Christian Broadcasting Network saying they were trying to get CBN news correspondent Gary Lane an interview with President Museveni. When they called Museveni's office, the people there told them, "Sam Childers is the guy you need to get you in and out of the country," and gave them my number. I set up their trip, including an interview with the president. I didn't know then that I would get to spend time with the president too. Not only that, he and I would have a one-on-one conversation.

The presidential residence, State House, is in Entebbe, south of Kampala on Lake Victoria. As we turned up the short driveway, we saw a huge, white, two-story residence with big wings on both sides and a covered porch over the center entrance, where our driver stopped in front of the staff member waiting for us. We walked up a short, wide flight of stairs and through the main door. The rooms inside had high ceilings and bright colors—red carpets, white furniture, and elegant red, green, and gold drapes tied back at tall windows where the equatorial sun streamed through. After a short wait, President Museveni came into the room and greeted us warmly. The president has a full face, a shaved head, a gray mustache, a big smile, and large friendly eyes that both reflect his love for his people and conceal a steely sense of purpose.

As usual, he was wearing a Western-style business suit for his interview.

I shook the president's hand and said, "Mr. President, I'm Sam Childers. Do you know who I am?"

He smiled his big smile and said, "Of course I know who you are. You're the reverend from the north. I know you very well." Uganda is about the size of Oregon. You don't go there and do what I do without attracting the government's attention.

I sometimes went to the front lines and preached to the Ugandan soldiers before they went into battle. The size of the groups varied from a handful to maybe three hundred tall, lanky African men dressed in camo and holding their AKs and RPG launchers, standing and sitting around in a clearing. I saw concentration and concern in their eyes but no fear, as I spoke to them about God's love and protection. One underequipped company had come back a few days after I spoke to them, marching and shouting and singing praise songs. I was at their camp and heard them a long way off. Three hundred fearless men singing at the top of their lungs is one of the most incredible sounds in the world. If we'd had a roof, the singing would have rattled it. Along with the singing I heard heavy engines, followed by the clank of tank treads. They had captured tanks and a big supply of ammo. They'd gone in with confidence and little else, yet all their needs had been supplied.

I had seen President Museveni from a distance once in Gulu when my men and I had just come back from Sudan. The law in Uganda says whenever we come back from

Sudan we have to turn in our weapons at the army barracks in Gulu. President Museveni was speaking at the barracks that day, and when I got out of the truck I was only fifty or sixty feet away from him.

Sam and soldiers back in 2004 on the front lines looking for LRA

So when a truck pulled up with Sudanese soldiers—one white guy and the rest black—all carrying machine guns and dressed in camo, what was the president to say? "Who's the white guy?" He knew who I was long before I knew him.

The crew set up their lights, turned on the camera, and Gary got his interview. The big excitement for me, though, came after the interview with CBN when my soldier Deng and I got to have a one-on-one conversation with the president. He was interested in my work with the orphans and wanted to assure me he thought the LRA was on the ropes and would be beaten soon. Like all presidents, he talked as though the war was over and won, though it was years after that before the LRA was actually out of Uganda. The one thing I liked most about Museveni was that I could tell he was not going to be defeated by these dangerous, crazy rebels. He wasn't going to be backed down by the LRA or his political opposition or anyone else. He was not even going to be intimidated by a madman like Joseph Kony.

Hearing Museveni reminded me once again of my dad's lesson: the first step to winning a fight is intimidating your opponent before the fight begins. Some people can be intimidated very easily, but not this president. In 1970 he joined the Ugandan intelligence service under President Milton Obote but escaped to Tanzania a year later when General Idi Amin came to power. Eventually he helped overthrow the brutal dictator Amin, rebelled against Obote, and in 1986 was sworn in as president of Uganda after a series of military uprisings. He is a fighter and always has been.

Museveni is also truly a servant of Christ. Although he doesn't use his position to impose his beliefs on anybody else, he's always willing to talk about his faith. He's been a Christian since he was in high school. He told us that for many, many years God has kept him alive. But he said he walked away from the church at one time in his life because members, knowing he was a soldier, asked, "How can you be what you say you are? How can a gun-toting soldier be a born-again Christian?"

To answer the second question—one I'm real familiar with—I look at Luke 22:36 where Jesus says to his disciples, "He who has no sword, let him sell his garment and buy one." Jesus was not condoning violence, but the time was coming soon when he would be betrayed and crucified. What Jesus was saying was, "The world is about to change and things are going to get real crazy. So I'm telling you, you will have to stand up for yourself." I'm also partial to the Holman Christian Standard Bible translation of verse 37: "For I tell you, what is written must be fulfilled in Me: And He was counted among the outlaws. Yes, what is written about Me is coming to its fulfillment." *Outlaws!* I like that.

The president went on talking to me. "I backed away from the church because of what people were saying about me. But I never backed away from God." I knew exactly what he meant. Look at the Old Testament. Some of the greatest believers who ever lived were fighters who turned away from their Lord at times but did great things for him too. Moses killed an Egyptian and covered up the crime. Samson destroyed an entire army—with a donkey's jawbone, no less. King David was still a boy when he killed Goliath; he later fell in love with Bathsheba and sent her husband to certain death in battle. And the list goes on. I think God likes a fighter.

It used to be that our presidents in the United States were fighters like Museveni and other African leaders I've met. These men don't just serve their country; they fight for their country. Beginning with Harry Truman, every U.S. president was on active duty in the military until Bill Clinton was elected in 1992 over George H. W. Bush, who had been the youngest naval aviator in World War II and was shot down in the Pacific. Nowadays we put people in positions of leadership who neither fought nor served. Personally, if somebody's not willing to stand and fight for our country, I don't know why we would want him leading it.

There's no doubt Museveni has his faults and opponents. I believe he knows he has made some mistakes—some wrong decisions—but I also believe that those situations forced those decisions. He is a man of peace and righteousness and justice. He has shown incredible patience in dealing with the LRA. As I write this, a cease-fire is in place, but the rebels keep stalling on an agreement. The government has tried and tried to hold the rebels to a deadline. For over a year they've been saying, "This is the last day. This is the last time. If they don't agree on this, it's over; we're gonna come in and get them."

Museveni is being pressured to keep the talks going. I know what he would like to do—he'd like to wipe them all out! Museveni is a smart man who knows you can't tame a mad dog. But because of political considerations, because of pressure from the people, he's trying to keep giving the LRA a chance. If I were his cabinet advisor, I'd say he's given enough chances. Now he needs to rule with an iron fist. He needs to tell them, "I gave you a deadline, you ignored it, so now we're going to kill you all."

Another great African leader was John Garang de Mabior, who was elected president of Southern Sudan in January 2005 but died tragically only six months later. I loved John Garang. He was a brave man and a dedicated states-man. To me he was the George Washington of Southern Sudan. Like a lot of other people, I suspect John was killed because he was about to be too successful in leading the people of Southern Sudan to a historic level of freedom and prosperity. John was from the Dinka tribe, like many of my soldiers. Even though he was orphaned by the time he was ten, he won a scholarship to Grinnell College in Iowa and got a BA in economics there. He went to graduate school in Tanzania, where, as a member of the University Students' African Revolutionary Front, he met Yoweri Museveni. Garang spent eleven years in the Sudanese army, then returned to the U.S. for a master's in agricultural economics and a PhD in economics at Iowa State. He also took American military training at Fort Benning, Georgia.

In 1983 Garang led a battalion of soldiers to defect against the Sudanese government that was oppressing its own people, Christians and animists in the south who didn't want to convert to Islam as the government demanded. He helped start the Sudanese People's Liberation Army and led it for more than ten years, winning support from Uganda and other neighboring countries.

Omar al-Bashir took control of Sudan in a military coup in 1989, suspending political parties and enforcing a strict Islamic legal code. Garang and his forces stood for freedom in the south and eventually negotiated a historic power-sharing agreement that recognized the semiautonomous country of Southern Sudan. In a historic meeting on January 9, 2005, the Comprehensive Peace Agreement (CPA) formally ended the war between the Khartoum government and the Sudanese People's Liberation Army. Garang was named first vice president of Sudan and president of Southern Sudan. He was the first Christian and the first southerner to make it to such a high place in government. The CPA calls for independent elections in 2011, at which time the people in the region will decide for themselves whether to rejoin Sudan or be permanently established as an independent country.

John Garang is the reason why there is any hope of permanent peace in Southern Sudan today.

I had seen John speak to big crowds several times; he had heard about my work and had seen me around the country. In spring 2004 he invited me to one of the UN-sponsored peace talks leading up to the January 2005 agreement. I was completely blown away to get an invitation, but it wasn't as spur-of-the-moment as I thought it was at first. By that time, I'd been fighting and helping the Sudanese for seven years; Garang had obviously been keeping an eye on me.

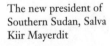

The new president of Southern Sudan, Salva Kiir Mayerdit

I had wanted to meet John Garang, and I wasn't too far from Naivasha, Kenya, where the peace talks were going on. We got a message to John and he told his people, "This is a good place for the reverend. Bring him. Let that reverend come to me." So I actually spent two days participating in the peace talks. Even though I had no U.S. government connection, I was a white American who thought his cause was good enough to come across the ocean and help fight for it.

The talks were at a luxurious resort called the Naivasha Simba Lodge on Lake Naivasha, about an hour and a half from Nairobi. It is a tropical paradise. The lake is surrounded by lush green plants, and if you stand there a minute, you may see a monkey or giraffe on the shore, a heron or cormorant sail in for a landing on the surface, or a hippopotamus or two playing in the water. The place is absolutely beautiful, with gray two-story buildings surrounded by luxurious green landscaping and even a few tall trees. Looking across the lake, you can see an inactive volcano, Mount Longonot, looming up through the mist. Flowers are a flourishing local industry, and there were huge, fresh, fragrant arrangements everywhere. The UN must have been writing a big check for all of this.

Deng, President Yoweri Kaguta Museveni of Uganda, and Sam

One of my most cherished memories of that time—and one of the things that touched me most deeply at the meeting—is what John did when I got there after the group had already started eating lunch. He moved the man sitting next to him and placed me on his right side to eat. It was so awesome. I sat down and bowed my head for a quick silent prayer, but John saw me and said to the people in Arabic, "Let the reverend pray." Everybody in the room— maybe twenty people—stopped eating, and I blessed the food for the whole group. Obviously there were a lot of non-Christians there, but it didn't matter.

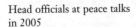

Head officials at peace talks in 2005

You could tell all the ones who were Arabs because of their *ghutra* (head wraps) and *thobe* (long robes). There were anywhere between six and twenty-five people or so, depending on the meeting. Sometimes we met out by the two swimming pools on a big stone terrace. There was mahogany outdoor furniture scattered around, upholstered in green with matching sun umbrellas. Other times we sat around the garden area in a sea of plants and blossoms. It was very pretty, but the longer I sat there, the clearer it was that humanitarian concerns were not on anybody's radar. All they talked about was oil. After a whole day of meetings, there was all this talk about coming to a final agreement on the oil revenue sharing and all that. But to me the subject of a true peace talk should be, how do we stop these women and children and civilians from getting killed every day?

I sat back and listened to everybody and kept my mouth shut. At this point we were sitting around a table out on a veranda, and everyone kept talking about oil, oil, oil.

I thought, *Let's talk about the children. When are we going to get to the children?*

The scramble for oil in Sudan is ruthless, lawless, and endless. Oil now generates 92 percent of Sudan's export revenue, but the industry remains unregulated and corrupt. The Sudanese government has no clear standard for regulating the industry and no way to enforce what little regulation there is. The oil companies don't care anything about the population or the land itself, and in the absence of accountability, they take advantage of both. The huge oil profits go to a tiny group of northern Sudanese elite.

Though Southern Sudan was supposed to get half the $5 billion-plus in annual oil revenues from four hundred thousand-plus barrels of daily production in the agreement, everybody knew the government of Sudan wasn't reporting production accurately and were almost certainly cheating on the numbers. All the while, oil companies were contaminating soil and ground water, and the government was driving the locals from their homes to make room for more oil exploration (from *Sudan—Whose Oil?* a newsletter by IKV Pax Christi, April 2008).

Oil was what was on their minds, and oil was what they kept stewing about.

When you're at a meeting in Africa, everybody goes around and speaks in turn, and you wait patiently for your opportunity. No interrupting. One of the hardest things about being in Africa for me is learning patience. Finally it was my turn. I wasn't an official at the talks, but I was there as John Garang's invited guest, and I had something to say.

I may have started off being a little more sarcastic than necessary. I said, "I thought this was a peace talk. All I'm hearing about is oil. It's an oil talk. I've been here for several hours, and I haven't heard anything about what we're going to do to stop the killing. That's what I want to know. I've come to hear what we're going to do about peace to save these children."

A couple of people looked at me like, *Who are you?* U.S. secretary of state Colin Powell had some representatives at the talks, and I heard they got upset with me. One of them asked somebody else, "Who the hell is this white guy?"

The reaction to my comment was a thumbs-up from people who knew me or knew of me well enough to know that I knew what I was talking about. Everybody around the table kept quiet, but I was confident that some of them were silently cheering me on. For political reasons, they couldn't say what they really felt.

There's also a frustrating tendency for African leaders to not criticize each other no matter how awful they are. At least I said what I wanted to say. Everybody else had to say and do what they thought was expected of them. I was not suffering under those restrictions.

Some of the participants approved of my comments, and some didn't, but I'd say it again. I've been in Sudan for eleven years now. I know the story. I know why we're concerned about Darfur. The UN could care less about the dying children in Darfur. Everybody's concerned about the oil in Darfur. It's not about the little black children who are dying. It's not about the genocide that has gone on for so many years. America is so blinded by the money and the politics, we add to the suffering by giving military aid to radical Muslim countries, even when our own economy is in trouble, like it is now. While the U.S. has had a trade embargo against Sudan for years, the American government sends this corrupt and genocidal bunch $140 million in aid a year. We are sending $140 million to a government that bombs and rapes and murders its own people. Go figure.

I'm a hillbilly from Pennsylvania, but if our country is in a recession and everybody else is cutting back, why is our government still giving out hundreds of millions of dollars to these countries? Why are we selling—even giving—surplus away to them? If we really want to have effective homeland security, let's stop selling and giving surplus of any kind to radical Muslim countries. Some people say this type of restrictive trade policy would be prejudiced, and America must not be prejudiced. Maybe there was a time to be generous, but in my opinion, 9/11 changed all that.

Those two days of peace meetings meant more to me than any two days I've ever spent in Africa. All the fighting, all the suffering, all the days I had malaria, all the days I had diarrhea, all the days I had to drink bad water, all the crap I went through during all those years in Sudan, it was all worth it for those two days. I got to see history in the making. And I got to speak from my heart to the most important leaders in the region. They may have been the two best days of my life.

During an earlier round of talks, Colin Powell had brought a plaque of peace, and it was put on a stone in Naivasha, Kenya, beside a tree of peace that was planted. I got my picture taken with John Garang by this stone. I spoke to John several times on the phone after that, but that was the last time I ever saw him.

John Garang at the peace talks in 2005

John Garang was killed July 30, 2005, flying back from a visit with Yoweri Museveni at Rwakitura, the presidential country home in southwestern Uganda. The helicopter was Museveni's presidential helicopter, an Mi-172, that went down during a storm carrying Garang, six advisors, and seven Ugandan crew members. At first he was reported rescued, then confirmed dead the next day. The official cause was pilot error due to inexperience in bad weather. Museveni had owned the helicopter for eight years, and it had just gone through a maintenance check and instrument upgrade. To this day some people believe Garang was assassinated. While the Sudanese government and the head of the SPLA believed bad weather caused the crash, others in the SPLA suspected sabotage. Museveni agreed that "external factors" could not be eliminated. Still others say that the pilot was paid off through the radical Muslims and crashed on purpose. I can say this much: they wanted John Garang dead. Not only was he an educated president, but he was a fighter. This man knew warfare. He was a threat.

Garang's widow, Rebecca Nyandeng de Mabior, said, "In our culture we say, if you kill the lion, you see what the lioness will do." She was ready to stand bravely for the principles of freedom her husband had lived and died for.

One of the saddest days of my life was when I went to Juba—now considered the regional capital of Southern Sudan—later that summer and sat at his grave. I had been so blessed by breaking bread with him and attending that peace conference as his guest, and in no time he was dead. His grave is in the center of a granite platform, a raised rectangle covered with some kind of light-colored tiles or square-cut stones and a pavilion overhead to shade out the tropical sun. There's a bigger-than-life photo of Garang on an easel at either end, and the grave is always heaped with fresh flowers. An SPLA honor guard is on watch twenty-four hours a day, a half dozen or so young soldiers dressed in fatigues holding their AKs at their sides. They take turns resting, sitting in blue plastic chairs under the edge of the pavilion.

I sat at his grave and cried for my missing friend and for all the lost opportunities. God is good and God is sovereign, but sometimes he's so hard to understand.

Salva Kiir Mayardit, a longtime friend of John Garang and another founding member of the SPLA in 1983, took his place as president of Southern Sudan and first vice president of Sudan. He was head of the SPLA when Garang died, and was sworn in on August 11, less than two weeks after the crash. As well respected as Garang was, some of the locals in Southern Sudan now like Kiir even more because he strongly supports full independence for the South, compared with Garang, who was content with the idea of southern autonomy within Sudan. Kiir met twice with President Bush at the White House to solicit increased American support for an independent Southern Sudan. Though the peace agreement was signed in 2005, it still hasn't been put completely into effect.

Kiir wants northern soldiers out of the south and more control over southern oil-producing areas near the Sudan/Southern Sudan border. It's no surprise that the Khartoum-backed Southern Sudan United Democratic Alliance (SSUDA) kicked up a fuss about Kiir encouraging President Bush to impose sanctions on Sudan. They claimed, "Kiir and his SPLM are masterminds of advocating for destruction of Sudan" (*Sudan Tribune*, June 6, 2007) in an attempt "to divide the peoples of Sudan in order to realize their colonial dreams."

However you look at it, governments around the world seem to be more worried about oil rights than human rights. And what about all these celebrities showing up in Africa?

Their hearts may be in the right place, but what good are they going to do in Darfur? I hear of celebrities giving away hundreds of thousands of dollars to organizations that put a little bit of money into refugee or Internally Displaced Persons (IDP) camps, and spend the rest paying their employees unbelievable amounts of money. What I have to say to all these big-shot celebrities is, "Get involved with somebody that's doing something!"

The refugee camps I've seen don't need foreign workers making big salaries to take care of people. The care workers in Sudan know just as much about nutrition and malaria and getting rid of diarrhea as the NGO experts there making twice or quadruple their salary. And then the NGO workers have to have all sorts of expert support: directors of development, program coordinators, volunteer coordinators. The countless administrative assistants make an average of more than thirty thousand dollars a year plus benefits. The average director of development—a guy in charge of fund-raising, of which there are many—makes seventy-five thousand.

The way these NGOs pay the locals causes a whole other round of trouble. If the average driver in Uganda makes a hundred dollars a month, and all of a sudden you pay him five hundred dollars for the same work, you have a bunch of jealous drivers. Local employers lose all their help because they quit to work for the relief agencies, and the cost of things goes through the roof. I've seen goats go from fifteen dollars each to seventy-five dollars each, just to cash in on the salary spikes. It creates a world of problems and hard feelings in the local economy.

If they have the medicine and equipment, local workers are 100 percent up to the job. But all the medical help in the world won't solve the problems in Uganda and Southern Sudan. The only way you're going to solve them is by fighting in the field. The ruthless animals who are doing all this killing will keep right on doing it as long as they have breath in their bodies. Reasoning with them hasn't worked. Giving them money hasn't worked. Diplomacy hasn't worked. Accepting their empty promises hasn't worked. But I know what will work.

The only way America can stop the killing in Sudan is by going to President Omar al-Bashir, and saying, "Remember today's date, Mr. President, because from this day forward, nothing is coming in or out of Sudan. Not a bullet, not a match, not a roll of toilet paper. A complete boycott is now in effect." Isolate him; cut him off. Then our government goes to all the countries bordering Sudan and says, "We are cutting off every dime to anybody that even talks to al-Bashir in a friendly way!"

You want to solve this thing? Turn it over to some people who don't know how to do anything but fight. We need to quit talking, quit giving away money, and establish an airtight boycott. I get worked up just thinking about this! Look at the millions of dollars we give away to help these other countries that are floating on oil reserves, including Sudan.

Why are we giving them all this money?

Since the peace process started in earnest in 2004, the United States has given Sudan more than three billion dollars. This is to a country that bombs its own hospitals, murders unarmed aid workers, and condones lawless militias that steal food aid and destroy humanitarian equipment. We're telling al-Bashir we want the fighting stopped, yet we're still pouring millions of dollars into a country that won't listen to us. Why?

It all goes back to oil.

If we boycott radical Muslim countries in Africa, then American businessmen are going to start squealing and complaining to their elected officials because standing tall is going to inconvenience a lot of American businesses. We have to decide if hundreds of thousands of human lives are more important than making a buck. Actually, it looks like we've already decided, and the money wins. If I were in charge of the whole operation, I could stop the killing in six months, guaranteed. Turn off the money tap to terrorist nations instantly and completely, and that would be the end of it.

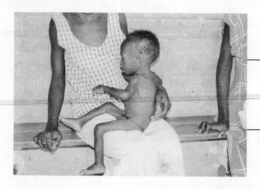

A child—whose parents had been killed—found in the bush.

Since that's not going to happen, we have to continue depending on warfare. As far as I'm concerned, the SPLA are the saviors of Southern Sudan. They're the ones who have kept the people alive for so long. In Darfur, which is in northwestern Sudan, the Sudanese Liberation Army (SLA) keeps the peace. These groups are real freedom fighters. The majority of them are Muslims who don't believe in the radical Islamic law. They believe in freedom. I have sat in meetings with the SLA in Juba, which will be the capital of the new Southern Sudan. I've supported them financially and will keep supporting them because they are there for freedom.

We have to bring al-Bashir's government to its knees with economic warfare. Life means nothing to him and his cronies, but money does. Not only does his regime send its army to attack its citizens, but it also supplies the Janjuweed, the guerrilla militias that are destroying Darfur. Bashir gives Joseph Kony free rein—the same Joseph Kony who was in the training camp in northern Sudan with Osama bin Laden. Bashir has homes that are worth $100 million, and while we send him money, his goons keep on killing. How many will die during the next round of peace talks?

While the talks and the waiting continue, innocent children are being kidnapped, killed, and abused. As long as that's happening, my men and I will be here saving as many as we can. Our children's ministry would never have had the success it has nor would it be able to continue without the help and sacrifice of dedicated members of the SPLA. While I've mentioned some of them by name already, I want to acknowledge all those of every rank who have played a key part in our rescues.

I've come to know and love the soldiers of the Sudanese People's Liberation Army from top to bottom. Lieutenant

General Oyay Deng Ajak and Major General Obute
Mamor Mete both have been especially good to me over the
years. I've been in bad areas at the same time both of them
were fighting. When I first went into Sudan, I was in areas
that were getting bombed at the same time Oyay was there.
That's one reason why the army leadership has always been
very supportive of me: I was there when the Antinovs—
Russian aircraft—were dropping the bombs. I stayed, and I
kept coming back.

Every officer and soldier in the SPLA deserves the
world's thanks for standing and fighting when it would
have been so easy to give up. Many people left Sudan
because they didn't want to fight for their country. Every
person who stayed behind is a hero, including the many
brave women of the SPLA. These women can use an AK
and fight just like any man. All those, both in the army and
outside of it, who have fought and sacrificed for the New
Sudan have earned the grateful thanks of everyone who
believes in freedom.

I also want to recognize and thank the men and women
of the Uganda People's Defence Force and other Ugandan
military units; the Sudanese Liberation Army in Darfur; the
Kenyan military forces; and any organization that fights for
freedom or supports those who do. In the middle of so much
turmoil, President Museveni continues to lead his people with
bravery, vision, and honor.

We should say a prayer of thanksgiving every day for all
the people who have devoted their lives to their country, both
those who are still serving and fighting and those who have
sacrificed their lives for the cause of freedom.

In addition to the men I've already mentioned, I want to acknowledge these as well:

Major General Jok Riak
Major General Willison Deng Wek
Major General Chol Thon
Brigadier General Edward Lino Abyei
Brigadier General David Manyok Byom
Brigadier General Kong Chol
Brigadier General Michael Majok Ayom
Brigadier General Riak Jorbong
Brigadier General Johnson Juma Okat
Colonel Igga Emmanuel
Colonel Louis Natale
Colonel Michael Mathe
Colonel Akol Majok
Major Peter Otim
Major Stephen Leim
Major Deng Wek Madut
Lieutenant Louis Tako
Lieutenant Samuel Majier
Sergeant Santino Deng
Sergeant William Guk
Sergeant Ben William
Sergeant Atem Peter
Sergeant William Deng
Corporal Lexson Night

The dedication of these soldiers has saved hundreds of lives. Without them, untold children would be lost and untold

families devastated. For years they have labored and sacrificed without anyone knowing of their struggle. That has all
begun to change, thanks to American prime-time television.
I had been trying for years to get some media attention for
our orphanage without much success. Then seemingly out
of nowhere, the media came to me.

ELEVEN
word gets out

The national spotlight shined down on us for the first time in April 2005 when the Christian Broadcasting Network aired the report I had helped them with, including the interview with President Yoweri Museveni. It was a gripping account of the carnage caused by the LRA. The report showed night commuters streaming into Gulu at dusk, bedrolls on their heads, then showed examples of the terror they were escaping. They interviewed a victim who saw her husband murdered before rebels cut off her lips and ears with a razor blade. Another woman, pregnant at the time, was forced to cut off her mother-in-law's hand to keep soldiers from killing the baby in her stomach. Then the soldiers made the mother-in-law cut off the woman's hand in return. There was an eleven-year-old boy whose arm had been shot off. Another boy, age five, had his arm hacked off with a machete.

CBN came to our Children's Village and learned the stories of Betty and Mary. Betty was nine at the time and had been so brutally raped she could scarcely walk. Vivid scars on Mary's back bore silent witness to the whippings she had survived. These two were co-leaders of our children's choir, gradually remembering how to laugh and play again, slowly healing in body and spirit.

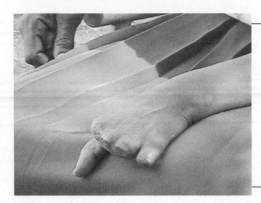

This young woman was captured along a road by the LRA. They made her choose between having her breasts or her fingers cut off. She chose to lose her fingers because she still had young children to feed.

As I told the reporter, "A lot of these young children have never experienced God the way we have. We lift everything to heaven because it's our only hope. And these children, all they know is their only hope could be us."

One fan of *The 700 Club* was watching the show on the road that night, and the story of our ministry got his attention. John Rich, half of the best-selling country music duo Big & Rich, was sitting in his tour bus relaxing in front of the TV before a concert. The story blew him away. The next day I answered the phone in my office, and a big voice with a Southern accent said, "Hey, I'm John Rich, and I'm a country singer. I saw you on *The 700 Club* last night, and I'm calling to say I want to help those kids in Africa."

John Rich? Country singer? Who was this random guy wasting my time with this big line of bull? I didn't exactly hang up on him, but I wasn't exactly polite either.

Two or three days later, I got a call from another Rich, this one named Jim. Jim lived in Tennessee and was a preacher and guitar picker who also sold cars to fleet managers. "I don't think you know who my son is," he said.

"No, I don't," I answered, "but I got a call the other day from somebody by the name of John Rich."

"He wants to help you," Jim explained.

I was unimpressed. I'd heard it all before. "A lot of people have told me that over the years," I continued.

"My son is half of Big & Rich. They cut Top 40 hits for Warner Brothers and tour to sellout crowds with Martina McBride and Tim McGraw."

Oh. *That* John Rich. "Oh man, I'm so sorry."

Not only did John forgive me, but he also overnighted a check for a large sum! That was the first donation our ministry ever received from a celebrity. We used it to buy a replacement food truck for the orphanage because the old one had just been RPG'd. John started to spread the word in the music world about our work. I actually had someone call me with the idea to produce a movie about my life. I thought, *Why not?* I signed a contract for a year to let her give it a try.

The real media jolt came when a major TV news magazine broadcasted a segment about the orphanage. I had actually contacted them about doing a feature but never heard back from them. Some time later they wanted to go to Sudan, and their government contact there told them to see me about arranging the trip and being their guide. Once we finally connected, and they found out what I was doing, they decided to do a story on me too. Sometime near the end of 2004, a production team came over with their correspondent. He has a commanding presence on the air with his compelling voice, square jaw, and flowing blond hair peppered with gray. Although he narrated the finished piece, he never actually went into Sudan. He stayed at our guesthouse in Gulu, Uganda, and sent his camera crew to the orphanage on their own.

On the evening of August 22, 2005, Lynn and I sat on our living room couch, glued to the television as the newsmagazine host introduced one of "the most dangerous places on earth to be a child."

The segment started off with clips of the night commuters streaming into town—a phenomenon the correspondent suggested "may be the world's most astonishing migration"—and an interview with a boy named Alex who spoke of the rebels killing children and their parents with axes and guns.

There was an interview with Jan Egelund, the emergency relief coordinator for the United Nations. "This is terror like no other terror," he said, describing the LRA. "I've been in a hundred countries. I've been working with human rights, with peace, with humanitarian problems for twenty-five years. I was shocked to my bones at seeing what happened there. I've never seen as bad. For me this is one of the biggest scandals of our time and generation."

Then came some historical background on the civil war in northern Uganda and Southern Sudan, along with the fact that the war was largely being fought with children. Joseph Kony had some screen time, bleating about God's wrath. According to the program, he believes he's a reincarnation of Jesus and Moses. I hadn't heard that before.

"In the end the sword will kill you," he rants. "The children will be taken into captivity, and they'll be burned to death."

They interviewed a boy who had to help kill another child who had stopped walking because he was thirsty. He beat his victim to death with a club. A girl talked of being gathered with other girls thirteen and above and distributed to rebel commanders as their "wives."

There were pictures of drawings the children had made—people tied up and bleeding, soldiers shooting, bullets flying. They showed a refugee camp where some of our children, maybe most of them, would live if we weren't there for them. Sixty-three thousand people lived in squalor, ten to a hut, malnourished and exposed to cholera, malaria, and HIV. Their villages had been destroyed, and then the rebels had attacked the camp and burned it. As bad as it was, risking capture in the bush was worse.

Patrick is a quiet boy of thirteen dressed in a bright yellow shirt. He speaks excellent English with a musical African lilt. He was ten when he was forced to serve the rebels. "We normally used a big stick to kill somebody," he explains, his voice flat and without expression. "For fear you must kill. If you refuse you are going to be killed." He watched his father murdered and saw his mother seriously wounded by knives. "Then," he continues, "they say that we must kill our mother. Then they said if we refuse, they are going to kill us all. Then we do that. I was thinking, without my mother, how can I stay in the world?" He looks at the ground and silently wipes his eyes with his shirt.

Then the correspondent got around to me, the "Lone Ranger" and "gun-toting preacher." Keith wanted to know whether I'd kill Joseph Kony if I had the chance. He kept trying to make me say, "Yes, I'd kill Kony," but I didn't say that. What I did say was that if I ran into Kony, "We're gonna fight. And I'm gonna win. I've always liked to fight," I added with a grin. "Still do. I'm a preacher, but I still like to fight." Keith asked if I was a missionary or a mercenary. I said, "A lot of people call me a Christian mercenary. I will accept it either way."

The report showed my soldiers and me joining hands and praying before we went out on a rescue. Dressed in full camo and carrying our AKs, we headed into the bush. I led the way in the Land Cruiser followed by our food truck, bristling with soldiers on this trip instead of beans and maize bread. The cameras revealed the grisly scenes of burned-out trucks and buildings along the way, including a school that had been attacked and torched by the LRA. Rebels had killed the teachers there, then cut one of them up and cooked her. Children who would eat her were let go; those who refused were shot in the head. The bodies of those who refused were stacked up in a pile. What the cameras failed to capture was the acrid, gag-producing stench and the electric fear that roiled around in the stifling air.

The segment closed with parting comments from Jan Egelund and Patrick.

Jan admitted sadly, "I have a deep sense of frustration because I feel that I'm failing. We are all failing."

Patrick concluded with an observation familiar to all of us who have ever been there. "We as the children of northern Uganda, we're so tired with that war."

The segment was over, and the network cut to a commercial. I sat beside Lynn on the couch, frozen in place. We were afraid they'd made me sound too much like a mercenary, focusing on the guns and fighting rather than on my heart for the children. I'd been going to Africa seven years by then, and that was the first time I'd ever let anybody take a picture of me holding a gun. Who on earth would give money to some pistol-packing ex-biker dude who might be as crazy as the rebel leader he was after? Who's going to believe in a gun-toting Good Samaritan?

Boy was I wrong.

The next day, so many people logged on to our Web site (boyerspond.com) that it crashed. Our e-mail accounts got so overstuffed they went down too. And just about every single message was positive. They weren't complaining; they were congratulating us! Pastors wrote: "We want to thank you for what you're doing." "Thank God you have the guts to stand up and do what you do." "I'd love to fight beside you in Africa, but I can't, so keep up the good work."

That show was the highest-profile coverage we'd ever had, and was one of many media accounts that raised our visibility to a whole new level. In time, Cornerstone TeleVision of Pittsburgh, TBN of Los Angeles, *The 700 Club* with Pat Robertson, the Mancow radio show in Chicago, and broadcasters in Uganda and Southern Sudan all picked up our story. I owe a huge debt of thanks to them.

Speaking invitations started pouring in from churches all over the country. We went from telling our story in country churches with fifty people to visiting huge congregations with two or three thousand people in the service. Within two weeks after the newsmagazine broadcast, I had received three hundred e-mails from people who wanted to talk to me about a documentary about the ministry or a feature film based on my life. Some of them probably had no clue how to make a movie, but some claimed connection with big-time Hollywood movers and shakers.

I had no interest in making a movie with any of these characters, so I threw every e-mail away. I had already agreed to work with this one lady who'd been in touch in the past and promised to give her a year to get a deal. Her idea was not actually a movie but a reality series. These were very hot at the time, and she wanted me as the subject for a reality-TV concept.

A few weeks after the broadcast, I was in Hollywood to attend a meeting set up by this agent-producer to talk about the TV show. The more I thought about the possibilities that might lie ahead due to the recent surge in national media exposure, the better my understanding was of the wealth of opportunities before us. But I still had several months to go on my existing obligation to the reality-show producer. As far as I could tell, we were getting nowhere with the reality concept. I might have just hung back and lived with it, but this was one of those times when life changed direction.

One day, after my commitment to the documentary agreement was over, I was back in my hotel room, and as I was looking through my briefcase, I stumbled across an e-mail from a producer in California. This was weird because it was one of the three hundred I had gotten right after the newsmagazine profile aired. I thought I'd thrown them all away. The producer's name was Deborah Giarratana, and her office was only a short drive from where I was sitting at that moment.

I don't know exactly why I did it, but I picked up the phone on impulse and called her number. What were the chances of a Hollywood producer being near the phone and taking a spur-of-the-moment call from a virtual stranger? A woman answered and I said, "Is Deborah there?"

"Yes, this is Deborah," the voice said back.

"This is Sam Childers. You e-mailed me a few of months ago."

"AAAiiiiieeeeeee!" The scream on the other end sounded like some sort of tribal yell. "No way! No way!" the voice shouted.

"Where are you?" Deborah asked.

"Well, I'm here in L.A. right now," I said. "I was wondering if you'd have time to meet me while I'm here."

"Yes," she answered. "How about right now?"

I told her right now would be just fine.

She dropped everything to meet with me that afternoon. Her husband came with her, along with two other Hollywood folks. After we all were introduced, I explained that I had a commitment to this other agent and her reality show for several more months. I couldn't talk about anything with Deborah until that time was up. We didn't talk or e-mail again for six months. Seven months after our meeting in L.A. I called her. She immediately saw the potential for a movie about my work in Africa. But knowing it takes years to develop a film project, the first thing she did was connect me with the publisher Thomas Nelson in Nashville and negotiate a book contract.

Later she introduced me to important Hollywood celebrities, including one Academy Award–winning actor who eventually donated ten thousand dollars to fund one of our rescues. I got the chance to meet him at a fund-raiser for the orphanage. We were at an unbelievable mansion in the Hollywood Hills with huge rooms, incredible views, and a crush of beautiful people all around. Deborah grabbed me by the arm and brought me over for an introduction. He said hello with that unmistakable voice of his and was polite, though kind of standoffish. I guess he meets so many people who want something from him, he's wary of everybody in the beginning.

Getting a movie made takes years from concept to finished film, so even if the movie does get made, I don't know how long it will take. They tell me six to eight years is not unusual. The good news is that our project is now in active development and has attracted the interest of some high-level filmmakers. That in turn has sparked interest in a documentary film that's gathering steam as well. As part of doing the research on them, I went back to some of my old haunts in Minnesota and took one of the screenwriters with me.

I'd been back there not long before to do the funeral of Delane Watson, my best friend in the world. It was so strange to see those places and look up my old buddies all these years later. My friend Norm Mickel is sixty-one now, still a pretty big guy, taller and beefier than I am. He has even less hair than I do, and what's there is white. When we ran together in Minnesota, nobody messed with us. After Delane and I left town, Norm was sitting in the Dutch Room, one of our favorite bars to fight in, and a guy came in and hit him in the face with a baseball bat. He was in a coma for two days and spent a week in the hospital. Delane and I laughed when we heard about it back then in Florida. We always said that it would never have happened if we were all still living there together. It's hard to believe Delane's gone. Conducting his funeral was one of the hardest things I've ever done, but that day some of the toughest, wildest men in town gave their hearts to the Lord.

Pete Barsness was a guy I partied a lot with in Grand Rapids, Minnesota. He's showing his age like the rest of us, sporting very long, grizzly mutton chops. My great friend Scott Wagner was there, along with his brother Bruce. I knew them both very well. These "Cohasset boys" used to hang around in Scott's basement all the time and get high when we were young, say twelve to sixteen. His mother—we called her Ma Wagner—used to holler down the stairs, "What are you guys burning down there?!" And the boys would holler back, "Shut up, Mom!" *That 70's Show* could have been written about the times we spent in that basement.

While driving through Grand Rapids with the writer a few months later working on our research, old memories came flooding back once again. Norm and a couple of guys had breakfast with me, and we talked about those long-ago times. When I think back about everything I did in this town, from fighting to guns to drugs, it's a miracle I am still alive and never went to prison.

But what about all the people I messed up? All the lives I ruined? Norm said, "Well, maybe you had to screw up some people's lives so you could save the ones you're saving now." All that sounded good, and it may have put a patch on my feelings, but I felt like crap. I began to think that revisiting the past like this was going to affect me mentally. I went to cemeteries and saw graves and tombstones of people I'd affected. They were just kids then. Jackie Evins's tombstone was there, a heart-shaped pink granite monument sticking up out of the thick, quiet blanket of January snow. She was twenty-five when she died in a motorcycle wreck, years after I last saw her. She was one of three girls already at rest in that cemetery whose virginity I stole. Another girl there committed suicide because she thought her life was over because of her drug addiction. I had put the needle in her arm for the first time.

As I stood there in the cold, staring at their names carved in neat, level rows of letters on the stones, I felt like I had to apologize to them. I was raised in a Christian home, but I had allowed myself to turn away from God. I had given them something strong enough to possess them and destroy their lives. Yes, they made their own decisions later in life, but I started them out on the road to destruction.

"I'm sorry," I whispered softly, looking down at the graves. "I'm so sorry." I wished I could tell them that no matter what happened to them or how old they were, each one of them was a child of God, priceless and precious in his sight.

To tell my story for future generations, I had to revisit this heartbreaking part of my past. What had started with a call from a newsmagazine producer four years earlier led to national recognition for our ministry and increased support for our work. That journey forced me to relive these darkest chapters of my past in order to share them fully and accurately. It also led to many wonderful opportunities to tell the stories of the children of Southern Sudan. Those opportunities are still unfolding today, and I think one of them is especially wonderful because it involves something I love only slightly less than my family and my ministry: a great big motorcycle.

Over the past several years—since the time I sent my mortgage money to Africa—the Lord has showered so many blessings upon our ministry from a variety of people. There have also been donors who wanted to give something to me personally or give a gift to someone in my family. A couple of years ago, a very wealthy man went to Africa with me to see the operation there and think about what he might do to help us.

His offer really took me by surprise. He said, "Sam, I know your passion for riding and I want to do something for you. I want to buy your dream motorcycle for you. Custom-built, whatever you want."

I laughed and said, "That's an incredible offer, but I've already got my dream motorcycle. In fact, I've got two of them." By then I had two fine Harleys in my garage, shining like new pennies and completely paid for. The being-paid-for part made them dream bikes even more. One was a Springer Classic and the other a Street Glide, both painted pearl black with drag pipes and lots of chrome. I couldn't imagine anything better for me.

But my generous friend insisted. "No, Sam, I'm serious. I want to build a special, one-of-a-kind custom job just for you."

I thought for a minute. "Can I do anything I want with it?"

"Sure. I don't care what you do with it."

I cracked a wide smile. "Okay," I said. "I want to raffle it off for the children of Sudan."

Now it was his turn to smile. "Done!" he said. "Who do you want to build it?"

There were a number of shops in the country that could do a pretty slick modification job on a bike for about fifty thousand dollars. That was not what I had in mind.

"Jesse James at West Coast Choppers in L.A.," I told him. "They're not an assembler or modifier of bikes. They custom build every piece from scratch. In the bike world, Jesse James is a legend." I was going to be spending time in L.A. on the movie and these other projects, so I could be there to watch the bike take shape.

My friend never blinked an eye, even after I chose Jesse's Diablo II design, which—at $145,000—is the most expensive bike he makes. The one change he made for me was to make the gas tank bigger and fatter, because I wanted to put a painting of some of the children I had rescued on the tank, and the original design didn't have enough room.

Day by day, piece by piece, the bike took shape in the West Coast Chopper workshop under Jesse's expert supervision. Though the sparks are flying, and the noise and banging are sometimes deafening, these people are true craftsmen who put art and feeling into everything they do. If you can't think of a motorcycle as a work of art, you've never seen the Diablo II African Bike. The finished product is huge, a chopper with long front forks, extra-wide back wheel and tire, loaded with chrome, fenders and tank painted orange and black with gold and white outlining. Jesse's trademark detail is putting .44 magnum shells stamped with his name here and there on each of his bikes. Since I often carry a .44 magnum in the bush, he added some extra ones to this job—on the riser, on the dipstick, on the wheels. Then there's the painting—done from a photograph and just as real looking—of three Sudanese boys I had carried out of the bush myself, looking up at you as you ride.

Sam on the new "African Bike" custom-made by Jesse James

Jesse caught the vision for our orphanage and the idea of raffling off the bike, and decided to help us out even more. His wife is the movie star Sandra Bullock, and he told her what we were doing. Sandra autographed the bike, and for the first and only time ever, Jesse himself signed his own creation too. Peter Fonda added his signature along with a list of other stars. All these autographs bumped up the appraised value of the bike to $350,000. We've hit the road, carrying the bike in a special trailer painted to match, setting up at fairs, at churches, and on college campuses all across the country, selling raffle tickets for twenty dollars apiece. By the time you read this, some lucky winner will have this one-of-a-kind bike all to himself. Unless, that is, he decides to sell it to one of the celebrities who has already offered to pay the winner the appraised value for it.

As the blessings keep pouring down, we continue to make even bigger plans for the future. But we still run up against many, trying challenges as we go, including fear, hardheadedness, and the Federal Aviation Administration (FAA).

TWELVE
an extra shot

As the newsmagazine, the African Bike, and rubbing shoulders with celebrities brought us more national recognition, a strange thing happened. Along with the donors who'd supported us faithfully over the years, we started attracting contributions from people who could afford to give away lots of money. The strange part about it was that some of these people who could make the most generous gifts were the most hesitant about giving. Donors who wrote those checks for fifty dollars or twenty dollars a month shared my passion for our ministry and gave even when it hurt. If they had a short month, they'd skimp on something else rather than cut their contribution when they knew the children were depending on it. That was a major contrast compared with some of the well-off people who were inspired at first by our story on the newsmagazine and CBN or heard it from their friends, who made big promises about financial assistance. Then they got cold feet.

Prospective donors with deep pockets came forward in the days and weeks after the profile aired and said they'd help us, then had second thoughts because of what I do—as if that weren't blindingly obvious from the TV show. They sat there on their silk sofas in their million-dollar living rooms—people who had never faced anything more serious than getting a bad table at their favorite restaurant but had caught a glimpse of what our organization does—and told me they were afraid they might get in trouble by helping me raise money. I wanted to say, "Buddy, you don't know what trouble is. Trouble is a platoon of LRA coming at you with machine guns spraying lead in every direction while you're having a malaria attack. That's trouble."

One very wealthy lady in California heard about the orphanage and said she wanted to give the ministry $100,000. She also said she wanted to introduce me to some big-time celebrities who were friends of hers, who would make big donations too and maybe even get their friends to pitch in as well. I told her I was planning to head deeper than ever into Sudan, to go deep undercover in pursuing the LRA. She stared at me for a second, holding one perfectly manicured hand over her mouth in surprise. Diamonds swung from the big bracelet on her wrist.

"What are you going to do if you don't make it out?" she asked, eyes wide.

I said, "There's going to be a bloodbath." Actually, if I go through with what I'm planning, there's a fair chance I won't make it back. I know I can get into the place I want to go, but I'm not sure I can get out. More about that in a minute.

What I hoped would happen is that this lady would say something like, "You're risking your life to save these children. The least I can do is give you a little financial support out of my idle millions. Why stop at $100,000? Let's make it $200,000! I'll never miss it. I spend that much on a shopping trip."

Instead, she called her lawyer. Based on his advice, she changed her mind about the donation. The best I can understand it, she became convinced that if she gave me money and anybody in the African bush was killed as a result, she could be liable for their deaths, and somebody could sue her. If her friends gave me money on her recommendation, her friends could sue her. I'm no lawyer, but my guess is that is complete nonsense. Members of our church back in Central City who scarcely have two nickels to rub together will give me one of them for Africa, but here is someone in a position to affect the ministry in a big way financially, and she gets jumpy about liability. I think this lady is a good person with good motives who was too worried about consequences and her own comfort to do what she knew was right deep in her heart. And I know after ten years of ministry that the only thing necessary for children to die and the world to go completely down the tubes is for good people to do nothing.

I believe if she and her wealthy friends really understood what was at stake, they wouldn't let a Beverly Hills lawyer scare them into inaction. They need to meet some of the kids in America who come up to our African Bike display, see the raffle tickets, and look at pictures of the Sudanese children in our orphanage. They'll say, "Sir, I don't have twenty dollars for a raffle ticket, but I want you to have this," then hand me all the money in their pockets. That's way cool. Those kids have their priorities straight.

It's hard to live in the bush and get to know the children

there, treat the wounded ones and carry out the dead, then come back to the U.S. and have somebody tell me, "Well, my lawyer says I shouldn't get involved." Unfortunately, ignorance knows no boundaries of class or geography. Even some of the people who come to see the African Bike have that same throwaway attitude. They look at the bike, look at the pictures of Sudan, then walk off and spend twenty dollars on T-shirts and funnel cakes. If only they knew how much the children over there needed that money and how much it would buy! Some biker will come up and look at the painting of the three boys on the gas tank and say out loud to no one in particular, "Who's the snotty-a-- nig---- on this motorcycle?" Who they are, are innocent children who have seen and experienced horrible things no one on earth should have to go through, innocent children my men and I carried to safety with our own hands.

When I hear comments like that, I have no fear putting those people in their place. My attitude is, if you've lived the experience, then you can talk about it. If you haven't lived it, keep your mouth shut. At a big bike rally in Pennsylvania, called Thunder in the Valley, a rough-looking biker dude swaggered over to our African Bike display and said something really rude about the painting of the three boys. I told him he was welcome to leave the premises immediately. I didn't use those exact words, but the message was unmistakable.

He got up in my face and said, "You don't know who I am. I just got out of prison." By way of answer, believing as I do that actions speak louder than words, I jumped out of the trailer into the guy's face and said, "You don't know who *I* am!"

196

He and his buddy who was with him took off, then came back later with two more of their associates.

I put my hand on my .45 automatic in my belt so he could see it and said, "See the pavement behind you? In about two minutes, there'll be five bodies laying there, and one of them will be mine. I've been wanting to die for a long time."

Somebody I'd never seen before came up behind them just then and said, "This guy's going to kill every one of you," and walked away. The four guys looked at each other, looked at the .45, and then all started talking at once. "Man, I'm sorry." "No offense, man." "I didn't know who you were." "Sorry, we didn't mean it." "Hey, let's shake."

My dad's trick of intimidation had saved me again.

The same thing happened another time when a truckload of guys started harassing me at a county fair where we had the bike on display. I went over to the truck and jerked open the driver-side door. The driver grinned one of those cat-who-ate-the-canary grins at me and said, "There's five of us." I looked him square in the eye and said, "Well then, I'll give you a chance to go back and get some help." They took off, and I never saw then again.

After that rescue when I had to leave children behind, I was on edge for a long time. I was fighting almost like the old days, but I wasn't the one starting the fights this time. I'd gone for years without swearing, and now I'd slipped back into that habit too. I was just so frustrated that I couldn't do more for the children, frustrated that I couldn't make people see how urgent and massive the need is. Beverly Hills matrons worry about liability risk, but they're not the ones getting shot at. They're not the ones who may never live to go to their daughter's wedding. The Bible says to put your hand to the plow and not look back, to forsake your family—even your wife—if that's what it takes to put God first.

If you knew there was a child in a building around the corner getting hurt right now and you could stop it, but ten minutes from now when somebody else could get there it would be too late, what would you do? Consider your liability risk? You wouldn't even think about it; you'd just do it. I'm always on the lookout for James 1:22 Christians who are "doers of the word, and not hearers only."

There are times when I'm disheartened by the church in the world. I take the African Bike to churches looking for support, and they tend to be lukewarm if you measure their response in raffle tickets sold. They have a sort of ho-hum attitude about it. Yet I can walk onto a college campus or into a barroom where they don't know about Jesus and tell them about Africa, and they want to help. I never had a young kid, a college student, a nonbeliever, or a drunk tell me he had to call his attorney before he could make a donation.

I don't mean to harp about the money. I had a ministry in Africa when I didn't have money, and I suppose one day I might face the same situation again, though I sure hope not. I've been entrusted with a plan for the children of Southern Sudan and the faith to see it through. That faith and nothing else is really the key to keeping our ministry alive.

Some days my faith seems so weak. Then I start remembering all the dangerous situations I've been in, all the people who have died around me, and think about how I've never even been wounded in all these years when I should have been killed a dozen times. If it weren't for my faith, I think I would have already been killed. And that faith is renewed every day.

I've seen cancer fall off of people in Africa. Seen a man with polio straighten out his withered leg. I've seen blind people have their sight restored. Miracles like that strengthen my faith. But sometimes I believe I'm a lot like Thomas—I need to put my hand in the wound. I need real-world proof of God's power. I think sometimes I lack faith because I want to be reminded one more time of that power. Miracles will do the trick.

Recently I was in California when I got a call from my daughter. A member of our church had been to the hospital, and the surgeon said she was eaten up with cancer. All they could do was give her something to ease the pain and send her home to die. Her family got her into a big cancer hospital in Pittsburgh. The doctors there said it was the fastest-growing tumor they'd ever seen. Two days later, on a Thursday night, I got back home and learned that the doctors had to operate within the next day or two because the tumor was growing so fast. I went to see her on a Saturday morning, and as they got ready to take her into the operating room, we prayed a prayer of faith like the book of James tells us to. James 5:15 promises that "the prayer of faith will save the sick, and the Lord will raise him up." We anointed her "with oil in the name of the Lord" as the Word instructs (v. 14), and prayed that God would touch her, heal her, and give her a miracle.

Two hours after she went into surgery, the doctor called me to make sure I was going to be at the hospital when the surgery was over. I figured he didn't want to be the one to tell the family the bad news and thought that was the pastor's place. I got to the waiting room, and when the doctor came out of surgery, he was really quiet. I was almost ready to pass out from thinking the worst. My faith was weak. I needed to put my hand in the wound again.

The doctor looked at me and the others who were waiting and said, "We cannot find any cancer." I said, "What? Are you sure?" The doctor told us again that there was no cancer, saying it could have been this or that. But he went ahead to say they went ahead and fixed this and corrected that, but they didn't find any cancerous mass. Two hospitals and five or six doctors had said this woman had a cancer mass that was fast growing and fatal. Now it wasn't there. I believe that God healed her. And in doing that he renewed my faltering faith.

God has even used me for healing. One day, in Africa, just as I was starting to preach, a woman stood up in church and started telling me about her niece who had a flesh-eating disease that was killing her. I didn't stop to think about where I was or what I was doing, but looked out at the people and said, "Let's go now."

About thirty people followed me out of the church to this young girl's house. I'd never seen anything like this disease before. It looked as if battery acid had been poured on her face, arms, and legs. I'd brought a bottle of anointing oil. My hands were shaking as I opened it because I was scared. I didn't know what was about to happen, but I had faith that something good was happening. I put this anointing oil on my hands and began to rub the sores on her legs. I closed my eyes and began to pray and tremble.

All of a sudden one of the women who was in the room let out a wild scream. When I opened my eyes, the sores on this young lady's skin were healing miraculously right in front of us. There are still miracles in the world today—they weren't only for Bible times. Seeing them and feeling God's presence are what give me the strength to go on with my ministry.

I need an extra shot of that strength all the time. Obviously I need it in battle situations. I need it when I struggle with living in two different worlds. But I never expected to need it against the FAA.

In April 2006 I was flying from the U.S. to Sudan on British Airways, the same as I'd done plenty of times before. Along with other supplies, I was bringing over some maintenance items for the generator we use at the orphanage to produce our electricity—three quarts of motor oil, two bottles of diesel treatment, and a can of WD-40 lubricant spray. I'd packed them all in a sealed plastic container and labeled it, just like always. But for some reason, this time airport security took them, said they were improperly packed "hazardous materials," and wouldn't load them on the plane. This was a bit of a pain, but we could ship everything some other way, and that's what we did.

I wrote a letter to the U.S. authorities apologizing for unknowingly breaking the law and figured that would be the end of it. Six months later, I got a notification that the Federal Aviation Administration was fining me twenty-eight thousand dollars. I called the FAA and was handed off to one of their attorneys, a lady who clearly was not having a good day. I tried to explain what I did, what the supplies were for, and that I didn't know where I was going to get that kind of money. Her response was something like, "We know what you do, and we don't care. This is your fine and you will pay it." I could have requested a formal hearing, but I didn't know that at the time any more than I knew flying with motor oil was against the law.

When contacted by news media about my fine, an FAA spokesman told the *Washington Times*, "Everyone is subject to the same standards. We are not zeroing in on one person or organization" ("FAA Fines Minister $28,000," October 31, 2007). He added that I could hire a lawyer and request a hearing.

When a reporter called me about it, I was sitting at home in Pennsylvania with Walter, the boy who had been shot in the eye and had come to America for surgery. I told the reporter about Walter and the fifty thousand dollars our ministry would have to pay for his care on top of a twenty-eight-thousand-dollar fine.

Help came to us out of nowhere in the form of a stranger named Hank Baird, manager of AllTransPack, Inc., a company that specializes in packing and shipping hazardous materials. He sent me government documentation showing that motor oil was not listed as hazardous material, nor was diesel treatment fluid. WD-40 was on the list of hazards but, he said, was less flammable than hair spray; it is the only item that should have been confiscated. News media confirmed the accuracy of Baird's claims using the Transportation Security Administration's published guidelines. (Baird also told me that a generator of mine that was new in the box and had been confiscated the year before was not hazardous because it was brand-new, contained no fuel, and ought to be returned. I haven't seen it yet.)

I did eventually have a hearing with the FAA. They decided to drop the charges on the oil and the diesel treatment and only fine me fourteen thousand dollars for the WD-40.

I told them I'd go to jail before I paid the fine. "There are people dying every day from lack of food," I said. "You are not the one that has to tell the children of Sudan standing in the food line that we have no more food today and send them home hungry, all because the FAA has given me a fine."

The FAA asked if I would pay the fine if they cut it again. "Before I will pay a fine, I will go to jail," I said. Paul and Silas had gone to prison for their faith by standing up for what was right, and I was ready to follow in their footsteps. The Bible says, "But let your 'Yes' be 'Yes,' and your 'No,' 'No'" (James 5:12).

The government attorney responded, "Most religions will usually come to a compromise."

Compromise? The idea made me see red. "That is the problem with most religions," I said. "The Lord Jesus doesn't compromise." I'm not exactly sure what the final official outcome was. All I can tell you is I didn't pay a fine, and I haven't been sent off to jail—yet. I think it would be really something if after all the years of heroin, cocaine, and LSD I finally got busted for WD-40.

Until they come after me, I'll be planning my next rescue, the biggest and most dangerous ever by a long shot. Right now I'm putting together the funding and making plans to go in deep undercover to document the LRA's most evil and horrific practices with top-of-the-line cameras, and carrying top-of-the-line weapons—little short AR-15s that shoot a hundred rounds, and .25 automatic pistols like the one I have on me now: the world's best equipment for five soldiers and me. There will be a crew filming up to one day from the transaction point and then I'm going to send them off with everything they have. I hope to come out so I can tell that story in another book, though that's up to God. But if I do make it out, I'll have film that's going to bust the gates of hell wide open for the children of Sudan.

THIRTEEN
worth every tear

War really clarifies your thinking on things. Makes it easy to see what's important. One of the reasons I like war is that you don't find many people arguing on a battlefield. There's no power struggle for resources and influence, never an argument over who's doing things right or who's helping the most. You can go to a war zone and pretty much work in peace. Everybody there is humble and looking out for the common good because their lives depend on it. But you get into an area where there's peace and everybody's doing okay, and there's going to be a constant tug-of-war between organizations. The safer conditions are, the more selfish people can afford to get. They bicker and argue and compete against each other. War shakes all that out of you.

War also reminds you of how little you have to lose in life, so you may as well go for it with all your heart. You can't hold back, can't worry about consequences. Life is short and tenuous, and the whole thing is a miraculous gift. Live life wide open, pedal to the metal, and you'll do more, be happier, and feel more fulfilled than you ever thought possible.

But shouldn't we count the cost? Shouldn't we exercise

caution? Luke 14:28 says, "For which of you, intending to build a tower, does not sit down first and count the cost, whether he has enough to finish it?" A lot of people who point that verse out to me think that since it tells us to count the cost before we do anything, we have to plan very carefully, considering all the variables and every possible scenario before we take the first step. Planning is an important part of all missions work, but it can become an excuse to do nothing; people who could accomplish great things are too timid to act because they can't see a complete and successful mission from the starting point. Or they're afraid of getting sued (can you tell that really bugs me?). They freeze up. I don't think that was the point of the verse either. The point is, before you start something, plan to hang on and finish it no matter the cost. The verse isn't telling us to not do something; it's telling us to set our minds and hearts on finishing a task before we begin it. I ran a construction company, built a campground, founded a church, and started an orphanage. I have no education and no special skills. But I promised I would finish each project before I went in another direction, and that's what I did. That's what anybody can do.

Sudan and Uganda are home to me now, every bit as much as the U.S. In some ways it's actually easier for me over there than it is in America. I'm as well-known in the Sudanese bush as I am at the grocery store in Central City. I was helping Sudanese rebels before helping rebels was cool.

In those early days it was hard crossing from Uganda into Sudan. You had to have a visa and also a special permit. The

Sudanese government wanted to know where you were going, what you were doing, and who you were doing it with. You couldn't just go into Sudan and start running around on your own; you had to be tied into somebody who was already there working.

When I first started coming to Sudan, none of the other nonprofits or NGOs wanted to help the SPLA. But I helped them with money and military assistance. Since I carried truckloads of food into places where nobody else would go, the story got around about this white guy who was a preacher and helped the SPLA in various ways. People got to know me, and as I would come up to borders, I would say my name right away. A lot of border guards would even salute me and wave me through with, "Go ahead, Reverend, go ahead."

These days I cross back and forth between Uganda and Southern Sudan and never have to show any paperwork. I always have a couple of soldiers with me, so most of the time they wave me on without even stopping. Because I supported the southern freedom movement, the army gave me a membership card to the SPLA. To this day I have an up-to-date SPLA card. When we bring teams in, the teams have to report at all the borders, but I hardly even get out of the car. Sometimes if I get out, I start talking with so many people I get tied up for an hour or so visiting with them. The people just consider me one of them, and so do I. I'm going to be there until the day I die; I'm sure of that.

Whichever side of the Atlantic I happen to be on these days, there's always somebody who thinks he can scare me or slow me down or even take me out. Just like when I was in high school, if somebody thinks you're a tough guy, he thinks beating you will make him the tough guy. In the U.S. I was being interviewed on the radio, and some radical Muslims with their noses all out of joint called in and started making threats. I told Lynn and Paige, "I don't want you to get scared, but I believe we could have some trouble at the house." I made sure I had enough firepower to take care of anything or anybody that cared to come into my house uninvited.

I got some short little 12-gauge riot shotguns—seven-shot, vented ribs—and put them within easy reach around the house, loaded and ready to go. I have ammo secured all over the place; our church is protected too. There are six armed men there on Sundays, every one of them trained. I wouldn't be afraid for an intruder to have a gun to my neck or my head. Any of these men could take him out at twenty yards without giving me a scratch.

The sound room in our church is upstairs in the back. The men running the sound equipment have TV monitors for surveillance cameras at the basement door and in the nursery. If I need to get down there in a hurry, there's a hidden door I can use. Unless you know the church, you'd never know it was there. I usually carry a gun on me, and there's another one locked up in my office.

The outside of our church still isn't finished. The insulation board is all up, but there's no brick or siding on it yet. The inside is all done. It's a high, wide room, almost square, with a stage area up front that has room for a drum set and all the musicians, including the singers. The three wide steps that lead from the floor to the platform are made of diamond plate steel. The pulpit is diamond plate steel too, welded together. It's the solid rock I stand on every time I preach. I like it, and the congregation likes it too. I'd guess that 70 percent of the people who come to our church share my type of background in that they're bikers, recovering addicts, or both, which means they tend to share my taste in interior decoration.

My wife always carries a gun. When I preach I never have one, but my wife sits right in the front row, and she has one. So I can grab it just as quick as I could grab one out of my side. It's not that I'm afraid, because I'm not. It's just I believe God gives us the wisdom and knowledge that we need to be ready for all things.

Even in my wildest years, I had a passion for fighting another man's war that continues to this day. I know now that Christ was working in my heart long before I became a Christian. I had no idea at the time, but God was molding me and preparing me to fight a real war overseas. The "wars" I knew before were between school gangs or drug dealers or turf battles in tough neighborhoods. In time, I got involved in a real war between African governments, between lawlessness and right, evil butchery and compassion, brutally brainwashed soldiers and helpless, innocent children.

There was a time when I fought in schoolyards, backyards, hallways, alleyways, ball fields, barrooms, backseats, orange groves, and pretty much everywhere else. That fighting was bad because it was fighting for the wrong reasons. What it did, though, was teach me how to fight anybody or any bunch of people under any conditions and win. I loved fighting then. And I still love fighting now. The difference is that today I'm fighting for the children and families God sent me to protect. Fighting for nothing more than the right for them to live in peace, worship in freedom, and wake up in the morning knowing they'll be alive and safe at the end of the day.

Blessings continue to pour down on me and our ministry. The Children's Village is the largest orphanage compound in Southern Sudan, and we're still building it, still expanding. Probably within the next year we'll be putting in a runway for our own airplane.

When I compare our situation now to what we were going through a few years ago, the miracle of it all becomes crystal clear to me. I almost lost my home; my stepson was killed; my wife had a nervous breakdown; my marriage was on the rocks; my business collapsed. Yet when I was losing everything I had, I still got up behind my pulpit and preached that Jesus is the only way, the only answer, and I did it with a smile. A couple of years later, when I told some of my congregation what I was going through then, they said, "Why didn't you ever tell?" And I said, "Because how could I tell people about all the crap I was going through and still tell them that Jesus was the only way?" I had to go through the storm with my head up high. I couldn't complain about the one I was preaching for.

And the journey has been worth every moment, every bruise. Worth every tear.

Those years of sacrifice seem a long way off sitting at dusk in the Children's Village today. When the sun's going down, it's the most beautiful thing you'll ever see. The stars start to come out, and even before it's completely dark, the sight takes your breath away. I've looked at those stars so many times at night all by myself, thousands of miles from home, and thought about how great it would be to have my wife and daughter to look at them with me. Sights like that mean so much more when you have somebody to share them with. The skies are so beautiful, and inside the compound fence you can feel the peace. Once the generator is turned off for the night, the world seems so dark and still, quiet and vast. It's as if God has spread a huge, soft blanket of protection over all the children and the people who care for them. Outside the gate, there's evil in the air. Danger and devastation can be hiding around every corner, in every clump of grass. But our compound is an untouchable refuge. The children feel safe. They greet the morning with joy.

Some of the guards that protect Sam's orphanage in Southern Sudan

PHOTOGRAPH BY KEVIN EVANS

The guidebooks talk about Africa being a land of contrasts. What they're talking about are the contrasts in scenery, climate, people, and cultures, among other things.

There's also a tremendous contrast between the safety of one place with another. There's so much beauty in some parts of Africa, but then you can be on a road to Juba, where ambushes occur so often, and your life can suddenly be in danger.

I walk that road with a gun in each hand, always ready to return fire from an attacker or sniper. Outside our compound, danger is never more than a step away. Yet every day I'm there, everything I do, is all worth it for the children—their smiles, their giggles, their runny noses, their innocent trust in a big-bellied *mzunga* with a pistol on each hip. Being with them, protecting them, helping them find their way to peace and a new life of hope . . . this side of heaven, life just doesn't get any better.

There's a special place in the human heart for children. Jesus loved them and used them as examples of his care over all of us and of what it takes to be a Christian. Mark 9 says that Jesus' disciples were arguing about which one of them was the greatest. To answer, Jesus "took a little child and set him in the midst of them. And when He had taken him in His arms, He said to them, 'Whoever receives one of these little children in My name receives Me; and whoever receives Me, receives not Me but him who sent Me'" (vv. 36–37). Later he added, "'Let the little children come to Me, and do not forbid them; for of such is the kingdom of God. Assuredly, I say to you, whoever does not receive the kingdom of God as a little child will by no means enter it.' And He took them up in His arms, laid His hands on them, and blessed them" (10:14–16).

Christianity is a hard path, but it's also a very simple one. Hard because we all sin and fall short of God's perfect standard. Simple because almost anybody can understand what Christianity is all about. You don't have to be educated. You don't have to understand theology or King James grammar. All it takes is an innocent, trusting faith that Jesus died for your sins, and that by confessing to him you will have eternal life. It's so easy even a child can do it. I'd say it's actually easier for a child than for an adult.

Not long ago I was at a rock concert, hanging out in the VIP room backstage where everybody was drinking and partying, and some of them were getting high. I had come there with a motorcycle group and was dressed in my usual biker gear: jeans, leather jacket, chain wallet, boots. If someone I know from Africa or your average middle-class American were to walk in there and see me, they'd probably think, *What on earth is Reverend Childers doing in that place? With all those people? He shouldn't be seen in company like that.* But that's not what Jesus taught.

During the concert, a woman came into the room where I was and stood by herself, alone in the middle of the bustling, crowded room. She moved around aimlessly on the edge of a dozen different conversations, looking down at the floor. Nobody came up to talk to her or offered her anything to drink. One of the partiers told me the lady was a big fan of this particular group, and she was dying of cancer. They had invited her backstage to meet the band after the show.

I walked over to her and said, "Ma'am, I'm a pastor. I know I don't look like one."

She said, "I know you're a pastor. Everybody's been talking about it, but everybody's afraid of you. They all think you're one of the Hell's Angels."

I said, "Nah. I rode with all the motorcycle gangs, but I'm a pastor. Do you want me to pray with you?" She said she did. When I started praying with her, she broke and started crying. She said that the last couple of months God had led her to this little church down the road from her house. "The prayer that you prayed is almost identical to the prayer that the man in this little church prays for me too," she said through her tears.

When I opened my eyes after praying, there were six or seven people crowded around us. They had all put their drinks down and they were crying too. "Are you really a pastor?" one of them asked. "What's the deal about Christ? Is he real?" asked another. The little circle of questioners expanded as others in the room angled in to join the discussion. I stayed there almost two hours, long after the concert was over, telling the story of Jesus to people who were hungry—starving—for a little good news in the world.

I don't believe you force-feed sinners. I believe you give a quick answer to the direct question and let it go. You give them time to ask another question. A lot of people think they're witnessing, and before you know it they're preaching, and that's why people don't go to church—they don't want to be preached at.

As I was leaving, driving through the field with the truck and trailer toting the African Bike, I started to cry and said to God, "You know, if people back home knew where I was tonight they'd think I totally backslid and walked away from you." It was as if Christ was sitting next to me, because I heard the voice say, *They thought the same of me when I ate with those sinners and tax collectors.* As we got a little bit further, I felt him say to me, *There were Christians at this concert tonight, but there was only one Christian who brought the Son of God with him, and that was you.*

If I hadn't gone there, those spiritually hungry rock fans might not have heard about Christ for a long time or ever. There's nothing wrong with a Christian going anywhere, as long as you take the right company with you. I've been in some rough, tough places these past ten years. Maybe I wasn't always ready and didn't bring God with me. But I know one thing: since that night I've never gone anywhere else without him. And I never will.

The whole way through this book, you had to make a choice whether to continue or not. Chapter by chapter you decided whether to go on reading or stop, to believe or not to believe, to begin seeing a vision for your life or turn away. Now that you've made it to the end, remember what I shared with you here—the pain, shame, hurt, forgiveness, change, and most of all, love for others. If I can change, if I can walk away from my old life, if I can become something, so can you. You've read about the choices I had to make to get here. Now don't put this book down without making the simplest choice you'll ever have to make. You only have to believe, not in me, but in the creator God who changed me.

Romans 10:13 says: "For 'whoever calls on the name of the LORD shall be saved.'" Have you ever called on him? If you haven't, say this prayer with me right now: "Father, forgive me. I have sinned. I have made a choice to believe in you. Amen."

Our sin is all about our past. I have cried many times during the process of remembering and writing down my story. But I cry for the past, not the future. Take a look at your past. All the bad and darkness, all the awful things that people did to you are behind you. If you can see your past, then you can change your future and do something good with your life. One man or one woman can help change a nation, and you're that one. If God can use me, think of what he can do with you!

I'm not saying there won't be hard times. But when those hard times come, face them along with the good times. In Matthew 5:3–5, Jesus says, "Blessed are the poor in spirit, for theirs is the kingdom of heaven. Blessed are those who mourn, for they shall be comforted. Blessed are the meek, for they shall inherit the earth." God loves you so much that he doesn't want to leave you the same way you were when you started reading this story. In his hands you can be a tool for working miracles. Since he created you, he knows every fault in your life, every bad thing you've ever done, every bad thought you've ever had. You think whatever you've done is so bad God can't forgive you? Then you're selling God short. You're defining and limiting his power. There's nothing God can't forgive, no sin he can't bring you back from. He knows your potential for good because he put it there.

Part of my story is what I did in Africa. But the far more important part is what Africa did in me. God used my experience in Yei and Nimule to transform my life.

When you look at my life overall, you can see that I was being prepared over the years for work other people couldn't or wouldn't do. Yes, I was tough and mean in a way that caused a lot of harm, but that toughness and meanness prepared me to survive in a hostile environment where very few preachers could go and come out alive. God was toughening me up and training me to be his man in Southern Sudan and Uganda. I can't reclaim the years I lost, but God can. The Bible tells us he can redeem the years the locusts have eaten, and I believe he's doing that in me today.

I'm living proof that you can salvage your life no matter what you've done. And not only can you salvage it, you can make it a triumph. In God's economy there is no second best. You are number one with him, and there is no limit to what you can do. You might even end up in Africa like I did. "No way!" you say? Remember, that's what I said too.

One of the greatest tragedies of our time is being ignored by the world. The devastation in Sudan and Uganda should create a global reaction, but it's out of sight, out of mind. Children are being brutally tortured and murdered by the tens of thousands, and all the world does is sit around and talk about it. Look at the pictures. How can you stand it? How can politicians stand to spend months and years negotiating and quarreling when children are dying horrible, preventable deaths every day?

Don't ignore them. Help them.

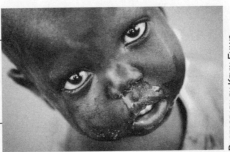

An orphan Sam rescued near Juba, Southern Sudan—the whole village was slaughtered by the LRA.

PHOTOGRAPH BY KEVIN EVANS

World governments, ours included, are more worried about oil and our relationship with China than they are about genocide. Whenever you can, steer the conversation toward people and humanitarian aid. Sudan is exporting farm products at the same time her people are starving and the United States is supplying millions in food aid. What sense does that make?

Orphans at the school in Kampala

Even better, come to Africa and help us. It will change your life. Maybe not as dramatically as it changed mine, but I promise you will never be the same afterward. These people need everything, and there's a long list of organizations on the ground in Southern Sudan and northern Uganda that need you. You don't have to have special skills or insights, only a heart to serve.

Now, I know that most of you for one reason or another can't make it over there in person. If you can't do that, send financial support. Money is almost always the limiting factor in determining what we can do in our ministry. We're working hard to be as self-sufficient as possible. Since we've had to learn to do everything on our own, we've started marketing those skills to other people.

Gula, northern Uganda—
children on the back streets

PHOTOGRAPH BY KEVIN EVANS

I've already mentioned how we earn money providing guide services, security, and transport for American groups in Uganda and Southern Sudan. I bought a well-drilling rig for the orphanage; now we lease it out to others so they can drill their own wells. We also rent out our houses in Kampala and Gulu to travel groups, and offer extra meals, sightseeing, and other services if the guests want them.

There are other ways to stretch a Sudanese pound. I am registered as a doctor in Uganda, so I can buy our medicine there, where it's much cheaper than in America. I bring donated drugs from the U.S. but never purchase any there for the ministry. I even buy medicine for myself in Uganda and bring it back to Central City with me because it's so much less expensive—antibiotics, malaria medicine, everything. Malaria pills here are as much as six dollars apiece. In Uganda they're a fraction of that.

In the Sierra desert on the way to Boma.

In the midst of all this, I'm haunted sometimes by the children I couldn't help. The ones I got to too late or had to leave behind. Not only would I like to have places for more children in Nimule; I'd like to see a dozen more orphanages all across the country. I already have a vision for the next one, in Boma. The fighting still goes on there every day, as it once did in Southern Sudan. A lot of it is tribal, based on old feuds and old conflicts that die hard. If the bike raffle brings in the money I think and hope it will, we'll build our second orphanage there. Soon.

PHOTOGRAPH BY KEVIN EVANS

Child refugees, Pabo displacement camp in northern Uganda

I can call people and bend their ear in hopes of a donation, I can talk about the children of Sudan in churches and

220

on college campuses and on *Oprah*, but in the end what I've had to learn to do most of all is wait on the Lord. It costs twenty-five thousand dollars a month to run the orphanage in Nimule, and for that we depend on hundreds and hundreds of small, regular contributions, though it's true that once in a while God lays fantastic surprises on us. If you'd like to give us a paper sack filled with cash, we'll be happy to put it to good use.

A child's toy car

PHOTOGRAPH BY KEVIN EVANS

The images of the children are with me all the time, burned into my brain, waiting for me every time I close my eyes. Once you see them, your heart will break, and you'll all of a sudden want to do anything you can to help them. Since you'll probably never get the chance to meet them yourself, I've done everything I can to bring the children to you by writing this book. No words can fully capture the suffering they've endured or express the unbridled joy they feel when they know in their hearts that *Tom-Tom* can never hurt them again. If I can only make you see how little it takes to transform their lives—a bed and a blanket at night, a full belly, clean clothes, and a toy or two to share—you will want to be a part of this miracle in our dusty little corner of Southern Sudan.

PHOTOGRAPH BY KEVIN EVANS

Children at the Pabo Refugee Camp in northern Uganda

I write with the hope that my eleventh-grade words will inspire you to give to this ministry with your money, your time, your prayers, your heart, or all of the above.

PHOTOGRAPH BY KEVIN EVANS

Refugee child—northern Uganda

Telling this story has been an exercise in trying to express the inexpressible. Everything is really too vast to corral and put on the page—the vastness of the African desert, of the needs of these children, of God's boundless love for his people. I've done all I can do here. Now it's up to you to say not, "What a book!" but "What an adventure of a lifetime! I want in!" So, come on in. I promise that once you feel—in the flesh or in your heart—one of these warm, tender, trusting, grubby little hands in your own, you will never let it go.

Acknowledgments

Many people helped make this book possible, and I want to thank some of them here for their extra effort and dedication. First of all is my wife, Lynn Childers, who traveled up and down some rocky roads for many years in order to help me do the Lord's work, and who has been my faithful partner throughout this book project. Our daughter, Paige "Sam" Childers, has also been beside me as the book took shape, and has done a great job keeping our ministry on track while I've been in Africa or huddled up with my writing team. I'm especially grateful to the godly couple who started it all, my parents, Daisy and Paul Childers Sr., who have loved me unconditionally through good times and bad. Thanks also to my brothers, Paul Jr. and George, who shared some of these adventures with me.

Deborah Giarratana, my manager, producer, and friend, has done a miraculous job putting me in touch with the people who could help me share my story: book publishers, movie companies, television companies, and who knows what next. She never stopped believing in me or my ministry.

Special thanks to my friend Brian Moats, who has been both a wise advisor and a generous supporter of our work. He is one of thousands of people in America and around the world who have supported Angels of East Africa and continue to expand its reach and vision.

acknowledgments

I'm grateful to the team that helped capture the story in a book: freelance writer and author John Perry, and editor Kristen Parrish and publisher Joel Miller at Thomas Nelson.

A special thank you to Kevin Evans for following me around and taking such amazingly powerful photos.

Though I mention them elsewhere, I want to again thank all the government officials and military of Uganda and Sudan, especially President Yoweri Museveni of Uganda, and President Salva Kiir of Southern Sudan. These are brave, patriotic men who have devoted their lives to improving the lives of their people.

Every story needs an inspiration. This story was inspired by the children of Sudan, especially the war orphans, who have endured so much and survived to be an inspiration to the world. God bless them. I give my life for them daily and consider it my highest honor to do so.

Most important of all, I give credit for this book and all that I do to Jesus Christ, my Lord and Savior. Without Him, none of what I do would be possible. With Him, nothing I do is impossible. Thank you, Jesus, for the joy of serving You.

Sam just outside of Juba in Southern Sudan

For more information about what Sam is doing in Uganda and Southern Sudan and to see more photos log on to www.machinegunpreacher.org.

Log onto **www.angelsofeastafrica.org**
for more information on Sam Childers'
current work and the Children's Village.

Your donations are greatly appreciated as
well as your continued prayers.

Thank you.